To Ask for an Equal Chance

The African American History Series

Series Editors:
Jacqueline M. Moore, Austin College
Nina Mjagkij, Ball State University

Traditionally, history books tend to fall into two categories: books academics write for each other, and books written for popular audiences. Historians often claim that many of the popular authors do not have the proper training to interpret and evaluate the historical evidence. Yet, popular audiences complain that most historical monographs are inaccessible because they are too narrow in scope or lack an engaging style. This series, which will take both chronological and thematic approaches to topics and individuals crucial to an understanding of the African American experience, is an attempt to address that problem. The books in this series, written in lively prose by established scholars, are aimed primarily at nonspecialists. They focus on topics in African American history that have broad significance and place them in their historical context. While presenting sophisticated interpretations based on primary sources and the latest scholarship, the authors tell their stories in a succinct manner, avoiding jargon and obscure language. They include selected documents that allow readers to judge the evidence for themselves and to evaluate the authors' conclusions. Bridging the gap between popular and academic history, these books bring the African American story to life.

Volumes Published

Booker T. Washington, W. E. B. Du Bois, and the Struggle for Racial Uplift
    Jacqueline M. Moore
Slavery in Colonial America, 1619–1776
    Betty Wood
African Americans in the Jazz Age
A Decade of Struggle and Promise
    Mark Robert Schneider
A. Philip Randolph
A Life in the Vanguard
    Andrew E. Kersten
The African American Experience in Vietnam
Brothers in Arms
    James Westheider
Bayard Rustin
American Dreamer
    Jerald Podair
African Americans Confront Lynching
Strategies of Resistance
    Christopher Waldrep
Lift Every Voice
The History of African-American Music
    Burton W. Peretti
To Ask for an Equal Chance
African Americans in the Great Depression
    Cheryl Lynn Greenberg

To Ask for an Equal Chance

African Americans in the Great Depression

Cheryl Lynn Greenberg

ROWMAN & LITTLEFIELD PUBLISHERS, INC.
Lanham • Boulder • New York • Toronto • Plymouth, UK

ROWMAN & LITTLEFIELD PUBLISHERS, INC.

Published in the United States of America
by Rowman & Littlefield Publishers, Inc.
A wholly owned subsidiary of The Rowman & Littlefield Publishing Group, Inc.
4501 Forbes Boulevard, Suite 200, Lanham, Maryland 20706
www.rowmanlittlefield.com

Estover Road
Plymouth PL6 7PY
United Kingdom

British Library Cataloguing in Publication Information Available

Library of Congress Cataloging-in-Publication Data:

Greenberg, Cheryl Lynn.
  To ask for an equal chance : African Americans in the Great Depression / Cheryl Lynn
Greenberg.
    p. cm. — (The African American history series)
  Includes bibliographical references and index.
  ISBN 978-0-7425-5188-6 (cloth : alk. paper) — ISBN 978-1-4422-0051-7 (electronic)
  1. African Americans—History—1877–1964. 2. Depressions—1929—United States.
I. Title.
  E185.6.G79 2009
  305.89607309'04—dc22   2009010040

Printed in the United States of America

∞™ The paper used in this publication meets the minimum requirements of American
National Standard for Information Sciences—Permanence of Paper for Printed Library
Materials, ANSI/NISO Z39.48-1992.

For my students, who continue to inspire me

Seeking no favor because of our color, nor patronage because of our needs, we knock at the bar of justice, and ask for an equal chance.

—Mary Church Terrell

Contents

~

Chronology

1928   Oscar DePriest elected to House of Representatives from Chicago
1929   Stock market crash
       Charles Hamilton Houston becomes Vice-Dean of Howard University Law School
       First "Don't Buy Where You Can't Work" campaigns
1930   Jessie Daniel Ames organizes Association of Southern Women for the Prevention of Lynching
       W. D. Fard founds Nation of Islam in Detroit
       Communist Party organizes Unemployed Councils
       "Atlanta Six" arrested under slave statute against inciting insurrection for organizing protest
1931   "Scottsboro boys" accused
       Alabama Sharecroppers' Union organized
1932   *Powell v. Alabama* (without adequate counsel accused cannot receive fair trial)
       Nixon v. Condon (no group granted power by the state—in this case the Republican Party—may discriminate on the basis of race regarding public elections)
       Organizer Angelo Herndon arrested for insurrection
       Don West, Myles Horton establish Highlander Folk School, Monteagle, Tennessee
       Franklin Delano Roosevelt elected president

1933 FDR assumes presidency, start of "100 Days" and New Deal programs
including:
Agricultural Adjustment Act (AAA)
Federal Emergency Relief Administration (FERA)
National Industrial Recovery Act (Section 7a supports unionizing)
National Recovery Administration (NRA)
Public Works Administration
Civilian Conservation Corps
Tennessee Valley Authority
Rosenwald Fund Conference: "The Economic Status of the Negro"
Second Amenia Conference
Clark Foreman appointed as Adviser to the Secretary of the Interior
on the Economic Status of Negroes; hires Robert Weaver
Robert Weaver and John Davis establish Negro Industrial League
Coalition of civil rights agencies creates Joint Committee on National
Recovery (Davis heads)
Father Divine opens first Heaven in Harlem
Adolph Hitler becomes German Chancellor
1934 Southern Tenant Farmers' Union organized in Arkansas
1934 Charles Hamilton Houston joins NAACP legal staff
1934 Democrat Arthur Mitchell replaces Republican DePriest in Congress
West Coast Waterfront (Longshoremen's) Strike
Claude Neal lynched
1935 Supreme Court declares NRA, FERA unconstitutional
Grovey v. Townsend (electoral parties are private groups and therefore
can exclude African Americans from membership and
participation)
Norris v. Alabama (routine exclusion of African Americans from jury
denies right to a jury of one's peers)
Conference on "The Position of the Negro in the Present Economic
Crisis"
"Second New Deal" including:
Social Security Act
(Wagner) National Labor Relations Act
Works Progress Administration (later Work Projects Administration)
Federal Art, Writers, Theatre, Music Projects
Historical Records Survey
National Youth Administration
Rural Resettlement Administration

Committee for Industrial Organization formed within American Federation of Labor

Communist Party announces "Popular Front": work with other progressive organizations

Harlem Riot

Italy invades Ethiopia

Mary McLeod Bethune organizes National Council of Negro Women

John Davis calls for National Negro Congress

1936 National Negro Congress convenes in Chicago

Jesse Owens wins four gold medals at the Berlin Olympics

Steel Workers Organizing Committee (SWOC) begins work

Socialist Party starts Workers' Defense League

Thurgood Marshall joins NAACP staff

Roosevelt wins in landslide reelection

1937 Farm Security Administration replaces Resettlement Administration

Joe Louis becomes heavyweight champion

William Hastie becomes first black U.S. federal judge

Bethune (NYA Administrator of Negro Affairs) organizes first conference on "Problems of the Negro and Negro Youth"

Pullman Company recognizes Brotherhood of Sleeping Car Porters

Herndon v. Lowry (expands free speech protections; vague slave-era "insurrection" laws unconstitutional)

1938 Southern Conference for Human Welfare (SCHW) organized

Report on the Economic Conditions of the South published

Gunnar Myrdal begins work on massive study of African Americans funded by Carnegie Corporation and WPA, employing dozens of scholars

Joe Louis defeats German Max Schmeling in rematch of 1936 fight

New Negro Alliance v. Sanitary Grocery Company (racial discrimination in hiring is legitimate labor issue so protests therefore legal)

Missouri ex rel. Gaines v. Canada (state must provide equal education opportunities for both races if it chooses to educate them separately)

CIO separates from AFL, becomes Congress of Industrial Organizations

1939 Marian Anderson sings in front of Lincoln Memorial

Popular Front ends with Hitler-Stalin pact

Germany invades Poland, beginning WWII

NAACP Legal Defense and Education Fund becomes independent entity

Hattie McDaniel receives an Oscar for her role in *Gone With the Wind*

Mills v. Board of Education of Anne Arundel County Federal District Court (state laws cannot set salary differentials based on race)

1940 *Hansberry v. Lee* (cannot bar African Americans from white neighborhoods)

Smith v. Texas (exclusion of black jurors from grand juries violates equal protection clause)

Alston v. School Board of the City of Norfolk Circuit Court of Appeals (Virginia laws differentiating teacher salaries based on race are prohibited)

Roosevelt wins third term

1941 A. Phillip Randolph organizes March on Washington Movement (scheduled for July 1)

Roosevelt issues Executive Order 8802: Fair Employment Practices Act

Army opens Tuskegee training school for black pilots

Japan attacks Pearl Harbor; United States enters WWII

1942 *Pittsburgh Courier* announces "Double V" Campaign

CORE (Congress of Racial Equality) formed

Southern Conference Educational Fund established

Race riot at Sojourner Truth Housing, Detroit

WPA ended

∽

CHAPTER ONE

No Strangers to Hardship: Black Life before the Crash

African Americans, freed from bondage but subject to segregation, discrimination, and violence, had nevertheless managed to find a foothold in the American economy and civic life by the 1920s. Black farmers tilled the soil, black teachers educated the children. Some who labored succeeded in joining existing trade unions; others formed their own. Black property and business ownership grew steadily. Local and national organizations struggled to improve economic and social conditions black people faced, employing strategies as varied as the groups themselves. African Americans served in local and state governments and had even, in the case of Oscar DePriest of Chicago, been elected to the U.S. House of Representatives. The first African American to receive a PhD from Harvard, W. E. B. Du Bois, did so in 1895; he was soon joined by a small but expanding community of well-educated black professionals. And an explosion of artistic production popularly known as the Harlem Renaissance brought the gifts of black writers, poets, dancers, musicians, and painters to broad and appreciative audiences.

Most African Americans, however, did not have that far to fall when the Great Depression arrived. Even before 1929, the vast majority lived in desperate poverty. If conditions had slowly improved in the years since emancipation, they had yet to reach the level enjoyed by most white Americans, even recent immigrants. By the time of the Depression, fewer than a quarter of black families owned the homes they lived in, compared with half of all white families. African Americans generally still earned less than whites, had lower rates of literacy, and clustered overwhelmingly in the worst-paying and least desirable jobs. Black Americans lived in a depression long before Wall Street's collapse in 1929 gave the economic catastrophe a name.

In the South, where most African Americans lived, the economic situation had long proved particularly bleak. No land or reparations had come with freedom, and most African Americans seeking to support themselves and their families found few alternatives to agriculture. The Industrial Revolution that had taken hold in the North had barely reached the more economically backward South that still relied on abundant cheap labor and staple crops. By 1910, just over a quarter of all black farmers owned their own land; most either rented or, more commonly, sharecropped land owned by whites. While details of sharecropping varied from place to place, the system always entailed giving the landowner a percentage of the harvest in exchange for use of the land, a house, and often tools and seed. Most large landowners who employed sharecroppers or tenants preferred the security of cash crops like tobacco and cotton, which were also relatively easier to oversee. By 1929, for example, three-quarters of all cotton plantations ran on tenant or sharecropper labor. The resulting overproduction of these staple crops, however, as well as overseas competition, led to lower prices and a decline in earnings.

Low earnings, in turn, brought greater pressure to expand crop acreage rather than invest in soil improvements that required either money or taking land out of circulation for a time. Tenancy itself also discouraged investment in conservation or improvements. Tenant farmers could not afford the temporary loss of land or the cost of fertilizer, especially when the landowner rather than the tenant reaped the long-term benefits. The failure to improve the soil, however, had unfortunate consequences for owners and tenants alike. The resulting decline in soil quality and, therefore, crop yield led to further debt and overproduction of a few select crops, renewing the cycle once more.

The overreliance on cash crops also meant sharecroppers could grow little for their own consumption and were, therefore, compelled to purchase food. While waiting for the harvest—and therefore their earnings—most sharecropping families had to borrow money to support themselves, usually at exorbitant interest rates. Any earnings remaining from the sale of their crops after the landowner took his share, then, often had to go directly toward the rapidly accumulating debts. When harvests were poor, debt exploded. As a result, many black farmers remained as tied to the land as they had during slavery in an economic system known as debt peonage.

In theory, their children could hope to do better. After all, they could attend schools or learn trades; since the Reconstruction era, public school attendance was mandatory for black as well as white children. The segregated schools they attended, however, ensured that black children would remain trapped in poverty alongside their parents. Jim Crow segregation, the practice of providing separate facilities for each race, extended into virtually all areas of public life. Despite African American protests and court challenges, in the 1896 case *Plessy v. Ferguson* the Supreme Court ruled such mandated segregation constitutionally legitimate.

Despite freedom, then, race in the postbellum South determined whom you could marry, where and how well you would be educated, what hospitals would tend you, and what seats you might take on streetcars or in theaters. It determined who would be served first and who last; what jobs and occupational training you might obtain; where you could eat, sleep, or use the restroom. Although segregated residential zoning laws were declared unconstitutional by the Supreme Court in *Buchanan v. Warley* in 1917, the ruling was routinely ignored or circumvented, and race continued even to determine where in a city or town you might live.

Not only were facilities segregated by race, in virtually every case those serving black people were clearly inferior. Privately run institutions or businesses either segregated black people or excluded them altogether; public services from hospitals to schools provided far better accommodations for white people than black. Segregation served not only to remind black people of their inferior civil status, but also to allow white people disproportionate access to public monies. Every dollar white legislators shortchanged a black school or hospital gained that much more for a white facility. With the systematic exclusion of black people from the polls through literacy tests, poll taxes, grandfather clauses, fraud, and intimidation, whites controlled the government at the municipal, state, and federal levels and therefore determined the allocation of public spending.

As a result, black education across the South was, in a word, dreadful. Underfunded, housed in decrepit buildings, employing underpaid teachers and outdated materials, black schools could not provide an adequate education for most of their pupils. Rural black schools often began later in the year and ended sooner, to free more workers to till the land and harvest the crops. When African American intellectual and activist W. E. B. Du Bois described the southern black schools he visited as "ludicrously inadequate" in *The Souls of Black Folk*, he was only reporting the norm.[1] Even Tuskegee Institute, founded by Booker T. Washington to train African American young people in agricultural, service, and industrial labor, began with remedial education more appropriate to primary school. Even fewer children attended school in the rural South. For every age and both sexes, southern rural black children were less likely to be in school than anywhere else in the United States. By the turn of the century several charitable institutions supported southern black education, including the Slater Fund, the Rural School Fund, and the Rosenwald Fund. Others included southern black schools among their beneficiaries. But even this aid could not approach the need, and, by and large, southern black children lagged educationally far behind white.

Close to a quarter of all African Americans were categorized as illiterate in 1920, almost double the figure for white immigrants and far beyond the 2 percent illiteracy rate for native-born whites. By 1930, black illiteracy rates overall had declined to about 16 percent, but every county in which black illiteracy remained higher than 25 percent was in the South. Most of the improvement in literacy came as a result of urbanization, not improved school quality; rural farm communities in the South continued to report high illiteracy rates for the entire decade.

School segregation did have its benefits. Black children learned within nurturing rather than antagonistic communities, highly educated black professionals who could not find employment in academia or their own fields taught in some of these schools, and teachers offered an educated and articulate base for political activity. Nevertheless, these teachers remained under the control of white school boards and municipal agencies, and they felt a great deal of pressure to conform to prevailing racial norms. Furthermore, no advantages could outweigh the entirely inadequate infrastructure of black education. In the South, and particularly in rural communities where so many African Americans lived and worked, school rarely served as a vehicle for occupational mobility.

Even had the schooling been adequate, job discrimination would have kept trapped black workers at the bottom. While not all African Americans in the rural South farmed, those who did not fared much the same. Many did housekeeping, chores, or laundry for white families. While this seemed less backbreaking than farm work, it was often physically grueling in its own right and similarly poorly paid. Furthermore, working under the direct supervision of whites, usually white women, proved just as degrading and demoralizing as sharecropping. These service workers remained equally dependent on white good will.

Both segregation and prejudice conspired to keep most African Americans in the rural South from white collar, skilled, or entrepreneurial work in white areas or businesses, but some found such work within the black community. Author Maya Angelou's grandmother, for example, operated a store in Stamps, Arkansas, that supplied local people with everything from food and household goods to cloth and farming tools. These stores served also as informal community gathering places where people met to talk, discuss the day's events, and enjoy each other's company away from the scrutiny of white people. Others served their communities through the ministry, barbering, doctoring, or preparing the dead for burial.

Black churches in particular provided a refuge from racist hardship. Segregation, divergent traditions of religious practice, and a long-standing feeling of racial community had created not only separate church congregations, but in many cases separate denominations. The African Methodist Episcopal (AME) Church and the AME Zion Church were self-consciously both Christian and black. Black Baptist congregations had begun forming their own associations separate from white Baptists before the Civil War. These congregations provided social spaces away from white eyes, aided the needy that white charities and government agencies neglected, and offered employment and leadership opportunities unavailable elsewhere. Some established colleges and institutions for educational training so lacking in the South. Although many black ministers were relatively unschooled, most were nevertheless powerful voices in their communities. Most of these men and women who worked within the black community of the rural South were marginally better off than the sharecroppers and farmers they served. Certainly they were more independent of white control. Nevertheless, the constraints of both racial discrimination and poverty operated everywhere.

Poverty encouraged a higher level of female workforce participation than in white communities. Enslaved African American women had labored alongside men, of course, but such coerced labor ended with emancipation. Given the precarious nature of life in the South, however, many black women joined in the struggle to feed their families. Fully 55 percent of black women in the United States reported having a job in 1910, compared with 20 percent of white women. As the example of Maya Angelou's grandmother attests, black women worked in the same fields men did. But they clustered largely in traditionally female occupations, particularly domestic and personal service. Two-thirds of all black working women reported employment in those areas in 1930. Gender, race, and poverty all shaped the black American work experience.

Beyond economic restrictions and legal segregation, white violence further ensured continued black subjugation, although vibrant community support systems helped mitigate some of its worst aspects. The Ku Klux Klan, originally founded late in 1865 by former Confederate officers and revived in 1915, sought to intimidate black voters and others seeking to control more of their own lives. While the Klan was the most notorious, many such vigilante groups, both organized and ad hoc, flourished across the South. Any black person who seemed to threaten white control, including business owners, independent landowners, outspoken individuals, and political activists, were targets. White mobs, often supported by local police and white townspeople, beat, tortured, and even killed their victims. Many lynchings were even advertised in advance for white crowds to enjoy. In other situations, secrecy better suited these vigilantes' needs, and black people they perceived as insufficiently subservient might be dragged from their beds in the middle of the night to be beaten or murdered under cover of darkness.

By the turn of the twentieth century a number of national developments seemed to threaten white supremacy. Industrialization and the resulting social and economic dislocations led to a change in politics that historians call the Progressive Era. Its rhetoric barely touched on race, but the calls for legislation to promote human welfare raised for southern whites the troubling specter of black protest. The upheaval of World War I culminated in white-on-black race riots in both North and South. For many white southerners, women's agitation for the vote also threatened white supremacy. While some activists exploited racism to argue for the need to grant suffrage to white women, the issue raised broader questions of equity and democracy. Rural black migrants seeking greater economic opportunities encroached on urban white neighborhoods. New political organizations created to improve black people's status, like the National Association for the Advancement of Colored People founded in 1910, posed an even more direct threat to white supremacy by challenging the inequality of segregated facilities and limitations placed on the right to vote.

In the face of such perceived threats to their way of life, hundreds of thousands of white southerners joined the newly reinvigorated Klan and other white supremacist organizations. So did many northern whites—these economic changes were national in their reach, and the huge and ongoing wave of immigration from eastern and southern Europe provoked northerners to express their own version of racism. To them, these newcomers seemed uncivilized and not quite white, and suddenly southern white rhetoric about nonwhite inferiority seemed to make more sense. While white rural southerners remained the Klan's central constituency, urban and northern white support expanded the group's power and reach. At its height in the middle 1920s the new Klan claimed four million members. Among its supporters were well-respected political leaders, and in 1925 the Klan received federal permission to parade down Pennsylvania Avenue in Washington, D.C.

One consequence of such broadly accepted racism was that lynchings and anti-black violence increased again, primarily in the rural South. Between 1917 and 1926, at least 419 African Americans lost their lives to lynch mobs.

The outspoken southern black civic leader and journalist Ida B. Wells Barnett labeled such bloody developments the "Red Record." For her exposés of lynching and her careful debunking of the myth that most black men were killed for threatening innocent white women, she was threatened with her life and forced to flee the South. Although economic scandals led to the Klan's decline in the late 1920s, racial violence remained high.

Vigilante violence could occur anywhere, but most of the danger lay in rural areas where lynch mobs could usually count on local law enforcement officials not to intervene. The larger size and anonymity of cities also helped reduce the danger of lynching, although white mob violence certainly also occurred there. This relative safety attracted many African Americans seeking a better life. Various natural disasters persuaded others to leave the land, from the spread of the boll weevil that ruined cotton crops to a series of destructive floods.

Greater economic opportunity proved the most common reason for moving to a city. New industries offered work not only in factories, but also in the burgeoning service industries that supported them. Routinely paid less than whites in the same jobs, black urban workers nonetheless fared generally far better than their agrarian counterparts. Their children also had a better chance at advancement than those living in the countryside. More urban than rural children attended school in the South; northern urban rates were even higher. Urban schools could attract more well-qualified teachers. This fact alone drew many black families cityward, in hopes of bettering their children's opportunities.

Urban spaces offered rural African Americans new possibilities. But how to choose where to move? For southern rural black workers and their families who desired to remain in the region, close to family and friends, the increased use of hydroelectric power and the building of textile mills as well as chemical and petroleum plants made southern cities a desirable destination. The black population of southern cities exploded in the early twentieth century. The African American population of Winston-Salem, North Carolina, rose from just over 9,000 in 1910 to almost 33,000 by 1930. Other cities' figures saw similar gains, if not quite so extreme. Atlanta, Georgia, added more than 38,000 African Americans between 1910 and 1930—surging from roughly 52,000 black inhabitants to just above 90,000. Montgomery, Alabama, grew by close to 10,000 between 1910 and 1930, and Chattanooga, Tennessee's black population more than doubled in those same twenty years. By 1930, close to a third of all African Americans still living in the South lived in urban areas. In that year Washington, D.C., reported 132,000 black residents; Baltimore, Maryland, 142,000. The black populations of Birmingham,

Alabama, and Memphis, Tennessee, each approached 100,000, virtually dou-
bling the number of black residents twenty years earlier.

For hundreds of thousands, however, the dangers and hardships facing
black people across the South convinced rural migrants to move to northern
rather than southern cities. The rapid rise of industrialization and manufacturing in the North, with its need for unskilled labor, drew many others. The
curtailment of the immigration flow from Europe, first because of World War
I and then because of strict immigration limits Congress imposed in 1921 and
1924, meant new job opportunities for African Americans. When they
could, therefore, hundreds of thousands of African Americans fled the South
for the relative freedom and opportunity of the North and West in a movement so vast it is known as the Great Migration.

In some cases employers were so eager to attract southern black workers that
they paid the migrants' way. In others, family and friends traveled together or
followed those who had gone before. Between 1910 and 1920, the black population of the North and West grew by almost half a million, almost as many as
had left in the forty years previous. In the next decade almost another million
had joined them. To put it another way, in 1860 fewer than 8 percent of all
African Americans resided outside the South. By 1920, almost 15 percent did
and by 1930, close to 22 percent. In fact, more black people living in the North
and West in 1930 had not been born there than had been. Approximately 1 percent of the black population in 1930 were foreign born, primarily from the West
Indies. Overwhelmingly, these new migrants chose to move to cities. Close to
90 percent of all northern black residents and 80 percent of African Americans
living in the West reported residing in urban centers in 1930 (see Table 1.1).

Specific northern and western cities proved particularly attractive. Pittsburgh offered its steel mills, Chicago its stockyards and slaughterhouses. In
1930 in upstate New York, 1,320 black men worked in blast furnaces and
steel rolling mills; in Michigan 13,025 held jobs in the emerging auto industry. Chicago, Los Angeles, Newark, and New York City more than doubled
their black populations in a single decade; Detroit's black population tripled.

Table 1.1.   Percent of Black Population by Region and Decade

Year	North	South	West
1860	7.7	92.2	0.1
1900	10.0	89.7	0.3
1910	10.5	89.0	0.5
1920	14.1	85.2	0.8
1930	20.3	78.7	1.0
1940	21.7	77.0	1.3

Like immigrants from other shores, African American urban migrants found their new homes both better than what they had left and less than they had hoped. Southern cities might offer more security from lynch mobs, but discrimination and segregation continued to limit black residential, occupational, political, and social options. Those moving to northern cities found themselves in areas free of legally imposed segregation, but discriminatory and unfriendly nonetheless.

Not surprisingly, then, most of these migrants found employment only in the worst jobs at low wages. Still, many found them preferable to the harsh conditions and generally even lower earnings of farm labor. The largest group of urban black workers reported employment in service, followed by unskilled labor; both northern and southern employers preferred whites for skilled and clerical work. Service jobs included maids and domestic servants, drivers, laundresses, butlers, and handymen. Most construction and shipping companies employed black men and women as stevedores, loaders, porters, and manual laborers, regardless of their actual skills or abilities. Businesses and apartment buildings hired them as elevator operators. Others held menial labor jobs like road and building construction. In the steel mills they tended blast furnaces, dangerous jobs others refused. In his famous exposé of the Chicago meat-packing industry, *The Jungle*, Upton Sinclair revealed that racism played a role even on the filthy, disease-laden killing floors, where African Americans held only the most poorly paid and dangerous jobs.

Both cultural expectations and financial need led black women into the job market in far greater numbers than did their white counterparts. Generally more independent and self-reliant than white women, African American women worked long hours at low pay, just as black men did. But for the most part their work was gender segregated. Black women also found the bulk of their employment in service, but in this case as maids, laundresses, housekeepers, and seamstresses. Better educated black women worked as teachers and sometimes social workers, shop clerks, or, in rare cases, businesswomen. Madame C. J. Walker, for example, built a financial empire on hair and skin products for African American women, and she used large portions of her significant fortune to support black artists and writers. Most black women, however, like most black men, remained in unskilled jobs with little hope of advancement.

Certainly the inadequacy of southern education hurt many of these job seekers. But even those with education and urban skills fared more poorly than their abilities warranted. Northern migrants did better than their southern counterparts, making up approximately 9 percent of all male skilled workers in 1930, compared with 3 to 4 percent in the South. Nonetheless, almost a third of all black male skilled workers in the North and West reported themselves unable to find a job at the appropriate level.

Those low figures for skilled work did vary significantly from place to place. In Birmingham, where the iron and steel industries found a home, black workers constituted more than 20 percent of the skilled labor force. Their proportion was similarly high in Memphis and in Jacksonville, Florida, where they were concentrated primarily in the building trades and railroad work. In Louisville, Kentucky, and Dallas, Texas, by contrast, black men made up less than 5 percent of all men holding skilled positions. Black mechanics, carpenters, and metalworkers could all be found in most cities.

Yet, although the numbers of black men in skilled jobs increased over time in both the North and South, their overall representation in certain professions changed little if at all. For example, while the number of black building painters almost doubled between 1920 and 1930, their proportion of all building painters rose less than half of one percentage point. The number of black bricklayers rose in those same years but their proportion of all bricklayers declined. The growth of black skilled jobs represented an increase in the number of jobs, not greater access to skilled jobs for black workers. Nevertheless, these employment gains were quite meaningful to the families of those men, as their income and status rose along with their job class.

As a result of such discriminatory practices, black earnings in each job category and for both sexes trailed those of both native-born white workers and white immigrants. Low wages and the high costs of living in a city left most black families desperately poor. Living conditions were equally unsatisfactory. Small black communities turned into ghettos as newcomers crowded inside existing neighborhoods. Most white landlords had long refused to rent or sell to African Americans unless they could not find white tenants, so black neighborhoods were located in the least desirable areas. They were therefore already crowded and dilapidated, poorly served by municipal agencies or private white charities. These communities declined further with the extensive in-migration, as overcrowding and continued municipal neglect raised crime and illness rates still higher.

Still, cities did provide other opportunities for struggling black workers as important locations for labor organizing. Although most trade unions excluded African American workers from membership, black attempts to integrate unions, or to form their own unions, took place primarily in urban areas where concentrations of black workers proved great enough to have hope of success. Perhaps the most fruitful of these efforts, and the most well known, was the Brotherhood of Sleeping Car Porters. The Pullman Company employed African Americans as porters on its railway trains. Although wages were dreadful and mobility impossible, the availability of jobs and the promise of tips lured thousands, even those with skills and extensive education. But the poor pay and degrading work provoked protests among the porters, and the fledgling union hired the charismatic Socialist A. Philip Randolph in 1925 to organize frustrated workers. Progress was slow—by the time of Franklin Roosevelt's entry into the White House the BSCP had only 658 official members. But Randolph's activism and the publicity he generated raised the issue of black labor rights in both the union parent body, the American Federation of Labor, and in the public eye.

The year Randolph began his work with the Pullman porters proved an important one for black union organizing. The National Urban League (NUL) established a Department of Industrial Relations under T. Arnold Hill to address black employment and organizing concerns. Frank Crosswaith set up the Socialist Trade Union Committee for Organizing Negro Workers, which brought together progressive white unionists with black leaders and civil rights groups to press unions to organize black workers and to persuade black workers to see unions as allies rather than antagonists. The Communist Party, convinced that racism divided a working class that should instead unite against capitalists, organized the American Negro Labor Congress. It linked black unionists and the International Labor Defense, a legal committee that took up (among other things) cases of racism. None of these efforts made much headway facing down white racist employers and union members, but they set the stage for greater activism once new legislation that protected organizing emerged as part of the New Deal.

On the other hand, black workers more often found jobs serving as strikebreakers when whites tried to organize unions. Employers seized the opportunity to obtain inexpensive replacements. In most cases those unions themselves had excluded or segregated black workers, so strikebreaking offered one of the few entrees into such jobs. The resulting mutual distrust between black people and white-controlled unions hampered later organizing efforts.

Not all black urban workers had to concern themselves with white employers or co-workers. As in rural areas, a significant number of black urbanites worked within the black community, operating grocery stores, hair salons, restaurants, barber shops, clubs, and the like. Black ministers, doctors, and undertakers served black clientele as did a number of journalists. With larger black populations, opportunities for entrepreneurship were that much greater. More concentrated populations of black people, and a higher proportion among them of educated and skilled workers, also provided more spaces where no white people were present. Dance and music halls, jazz and blues clubs, and bars flourished, where black people mingled, exchanged ideas, and reshaped black cultural expression.

Yet the presence of so many social outlets also increased the likelihood of crime and what law enforcement termed "vice": prostitution, gambling, numbers running, and the illegal production and consumption of alcohol. Black parents who worried in the countryside about white violence worried if they moved to the city about the dangerous influences of this environment on their children. In 1928, African American sociologist Henry J. McGuinn studied businesses in sixteen cities that catered to the black community's social life and warned of widespread drunkenness, prostitution, and sex-seeking men prowling for vulnerable women. He offered specific examples from Memphis dance halls, filled with profanity, unseemly sexual conduct, and petty crime. Their real danger, he warned, was their attractiveness to black migrants who were segregated in unfit residential areas and economically exploited. Nevertheless, such illegal activities, while both dangerous and exploitative, also offered opportunities for black entrepreneurship. A number of black men (and a few black women), whether desperate or entrepreneurial, earned money in these ways.

Informing local communities about these issues were hundreds of black newspapers, made possible by the population growth, which served thousands of eager readers. Black Baltimore residents, and others around the country, read the *Baltimore Afro-American*. Almost 94,000 black locals made possible the publication of the *St. Louis Argus*. Cleveland's 72,000 black locals followed events through the *Cleveland Gazette*. Los Angeles's black community of close to 39,000 relied on the *California Eagle*. The *Gary American* (just under 18,000) served Indiana residents. Chicago, with more than 230,000 African American residents in 1930, supported the *Defender*, so widely read that it published northern job advertisements for its southern readers. New York's black community of 327,000 was so large that it could support two major newspapers, the *Amsterdam News* and the *New York Age*, as well as several smaller ones. The *Birmingham Reporter* (black population 99,000), *Atlanta Daily World* (for a population of 90,000), *Louisiana Weekly* (New Orleans had close to 130,000 black residents), and hundreds of others in large and even moderately sized communities kept their communities informed of significant local, national, and international events of concern to black people that white papers did not cover. They provided an analysis of the news from a black perspective. They also advertised the tremendous variety of black political, artistic, religious, and social programs emerging in these growing black communities, thereby spurring black organizing and community building.

Indeed, black urban life offered rich social and political opportunities largely unavailable in rural areas. Church congregations expanded with the growth of the black population. Denominational congregations found themselves bursting out of their original spaces as their ranks swelled with newcomers. Thousands of independent and storefront churches opened their doors to those seeking a different religious experience. Fraternal and sororal organizations flourished, including local chapters of national organizations like the Black Elks and the National Association of Colored Graduate Nurses as well as local groups like church committees, sewing circles, and literary, musical, and community service societies.

Women in particular found a voice in communal organizations. Local women's clubs had banded together in 1896 as the National Association of Colored Women's Clubs (NACWC). Its motto, "Lifting as we climb," represented the benevolent and charitable commitment to racial uplift the association exemplified. Local chapters educated mothers about health care and nutrition and provided residences for single women, as well as clothing, food, and other necessities to the needy. These clubs, black sororities (the first, Alpha Kappa Alpha, was founded at Howard University in 1908), and many other such groups and professional societies provided many women with both social outlets and opportunities for service. Given the widespread poverty and illiteracy, inadequate medical care and social services, and segregated social opportunities, these associations found quite a vacuum to fill. To give some sense of the scope of the need, nationwide in 1930 only 3,805 black physicians ministered to a total black population of close to 12 million, most of whom lacked access to white doctors.

To the extent that these associations acted in the public sphere, they by and large utilized Booker T. Washington's self-help goals and accomodationist style. In this they were joined by other interracial groups also dedicated to improving conditions through gradual and nonconfrontational steps. Primarily staffed by middle-class people, groups like the Colored YMCA and the NUL, like the NACWC, sought to assimilate black migrants into urban life and minimize white racism by promoting lifestyles and values they believed best suited for success. Urban League handbills advised newcomers to get a job quickly and show up for work every day. The *Defender* urged men not to speak or laugh loudly in public, or make salacious comments about women.

Generally wise advice, it could also come across as paternalistic and elitist. Mary Church Terrell, first president of the NACWC, called upon members to "inculcate correct principles, and set good examples" for the "little strays of the alleys" who needed to "come in contact with intelligence and virtue, at least a few times a week."[2] Nevertheless, these groups met crucial needs by providing temporary housing, employment services, emergency economic aid, and the like to new migrants poorly served by white charitable agencies. By 1925, for example, the Urban League had fifty-one local branches, working to settle new migrants and their families, find them jobs, train them in new skills, and encourage white employers to hire them.

Some of these agencies, like the NUL, the National Federation of Settlements, and the YWCA, had both white and black board members and advocates. Other groups, like the NACWC, were all black, recognizing the indifference of most white people to black needs. Concentrating less on relations with whites, they organized programs to meet particular needs of the black migrant community from day care facilities for children with working parents to medical care, from education programs to care for the elderly.

More politically minded organizations followed the model set by W. E. B. Du Bois and others who rejected Booker T. Washington's gradualist approach. Arguing that African Americans deserved all the rights and benefits accorded other citizens, groups like the National Association for the Advancement of Colored People (NAACP) sought to augment self-help efforts by working toward the abolition of all discriminatory laws.

The association considered equal voting rights to be among its most important goals, since voters select legislators who pass or repeal laws. Since the end of Reconstruction, southern states had used a variety of tactics to exclude black voters from the polls and therefore from decision making. Grandfather clauses, for example, permitted anyone otherwise disenfranchised to vote if that individual's grandfather had enjoyed that right. This law clearly intended to exclude African Americans, who had only recently gained the vote. The NAACP challenged such practices in court, and in 1915 the Supreme Court ruled grandfather clauses unconstitutional in *Guinn v. United States*. In 1927 the NAACP won another victory when the court ruled in *Nixon v. Herndon* that states could not exclude African Americans from electoral primaries. Although southern states continued to exclude most black voters by various means, including privately run political primaries, requiring the payment of annual "poll" taxes in order to vote or outright intimidation, it was clear that an assault on the all-white political system had begun.

The NAACP worked with the executive and legislative branches as well as with the courts, pressuring the president to end discrimination in federal hiring and pressing Congress for anti-lynching and antidiscrimination legislation. Such efforts enjoyed only limited success. Few in power concerned themselves with African Americans, and the resistance of southern senators and congressmen doomed any civil rights legislation. World War I brought renewed energy to the struggle. The war's patriotic rhetoric that this was a struggle for freedom and democracy inspired the 400,000 African Americans who served in segregated units in the Armed Forces to expect equal treatment upon their return. Although this expectation was rarely met, the struggle was joined. "We return," the NAACP's *Crisis* magazine warned in 1919. "We return from fighting. We return fighting. Make way for democracy! We saved it in France, and by the Great Jehovah we will save it in the United States of America, or know the reason why."[3]

Locally, members of NAACP chapters and other black political leaders met with city officials to demand better services in black neighborhoods and more African Americans hired for municipal jobs. Although the threat of black equality provoked some of the worst white violence against African Americans seen for decades, black leaders continued to insist that the war's promise required equality at home.

The combination of increased demands for equal treatment and continuing competition for jobs and living space in urban areas fueled more than twenty race riots between 1917 and 1919. In 1917 whites attacked black city dwellers in East St. Louis, Illinois, killing forty. The NAACP responded by bringing 5,000 protesters onto New York's Fifth Avenue for a silent "Parade of Muffled Drums." Chester, Pennsylvania (1917), Houston, Texas (1917), Washington, D.C. (1919), Omaha, Nebraska (1919), Charleston, South Carolina (1919), Knoxville, Tennessee (1919), Elaine, Arkansas (1919), and other towns and cities suffered race riots of their own.

In Elaine, for example, black cotton farmers met in a church to organize a protest against white landowners who had cheated them out of their profits. They agreed to form the Progressive Farmers and Household Union of America and to hire a lawyer to challenge the planters. But a white mob surrounded the church and firing began. Five white and at least twenty-five black people died in the violence. Twelve black men were charged with murder and quickly convicted although the NAACP later won their release. Whites in Tulsa, Oklahoma, attacked black residents in a 1921 riot, destroying black homes and killing as many as 300. A similar riot in Rosewood, Florida, in 1923 killed and wounded undetermined numbers and burned the black neighborhood entirely to the ground.

Perhaps the worst racial violence occurred in Chicago in 1919. There, the riot was sparked by the accidental straying of a young black swimmer into the section of Lake Michigan reserved for whites. The child drowned in a barrage of stones. White mobs pulled black riders from streetcars and black passersby from sidewalks to beat them and destroyed black homes. They met some black resistance, and the violence raged for several days until the National Guard finally restored calm. In all 537 were wounded and 38 killed, 23 of whom were black. Racism outside the South might not have been enshrined in law, but it was deeply ingrained in social and civic life nonetheless.

Although the scope of political agendas and the likelihood of success were both greater in the North, southern black residents participated in many of these political struggles for better services or greater equality. In some southern cities enough black voters were able to join the rolls to form black political organizations, homegrown political groups that organized around specific issues of education or civic life. Sometimes local chapters of national civil rights organizations like the NAACP coordinated political efforts in southern cities, such as its challenge to residential zoning laws based on race. While progress was slow, the NAACP's legal suits began to chip away at the legal basis for segregation.

Because vindictive white employers in the South routinely fired black workers who engaged in any political activity, men and women who supported themselves through the black community were often in the forefront of these political actions. They could afford to take a slightly greater risk, as they did not depend on whites for their livelihoods. On the other hand, they also had more to lose if whites reacted too violently. As a result, and because the threat of white vigilante violence hung over every black community, urban as well as rural, most southern black and interracial political efforts on behalf of racial equality were moderate, polite, and private. The Commission on Interracial Cooperation, established in 1919 amid a spate of race riots in the hope of easing racial frictions, employed a gradualist approach that focused primarily on educating white people to the contributions African Americans had made to the nation. The group refused to advocate for black voting rights guaranteed under the Constitution, although it did speak publicly against white vigilante violence, particularly through its 1930 offshoot, the Association of Southern Women for the Prevention of Lynching.

Southern activists did occasionally join national antiracism efforts. After President Wilson's administration expanded segregation in government hiring, a delegation of black and white leaders in both the South and the North organized protests, petition drives, letters, and meetings with the president. Such efforts convinced the Treasury Department to dismantle the discriminatory policies it had so recently instated, although practices elsewhere improved little.

Such open southern black activism was relatively rare, however. In northern and western cities, where African Americans voted and no laws undergirded segregation, the same residential clustering brought greater potential for mass action. Evident not only in the self-defensive measures Chicagoans employed during the 1919 riot but also in more traditional political expressions, northern black urbanites turned their self-help groups, political clubs, and social organizations into energetic instruments for change. Urban Leagues and charitable aid groups, church societies, and NAACP chapters organized vigorously to generate greater opportunities for their community.

Black engagement in the political process often brought substantive and visible change. Because no voting restrictions existed in the North, and because black populations were clustered in small areas, black voting blocs had clout in heavily contested elections. In many of these situations, local black Democratic and Republican political clubs succeeded in winning concessions from potential candidates. In New York, J. Raymond Jones, the "Harlem Fox," built a political empire within the Democratic Party's political machine. In 1928 Republican Oscar DePriest won election to Congress from his heavily black Chicago district. In a number of northern and western cities black votes produced greater services for black communities or explicit antidiscrimination ordinances.

Such advances were limited, however, and white racism seemed to many, both North and South, to be impenetrable. Black nationalists, whether in self-help or political organizations, argued that the assimilation into white society advocated by both gradualists like the NUL and "immediatists" like the NAACP, was both undesirable and impossible to achieve. Nationalism had a long history in the United States, but the charismatic Jamaican-born Marcus Garvey brought the movement a new visibility and thousands of new adherents. Blackness was no cause for shame, he insisted, but rather a symbol of honor, evidence of descent from the earliest of civilizations. Garvey arrived in New York in 1916 and quickly established an infrastructure for his nationalist dream, the Universal Negro Improvement Association (UNIA). He formed a black-run shipping company, the Black Star Line, to further Pan-African trade connections, and called for the establishment of a black-led nation in Africa. He gave himself the title of Provisional President of Africa and established an African Orthodox church that worshiped a black Jesus and Mary. His many parades and public addresses, the bestowal of positions in the planned new nation, and his newspaper *The Negro World* ensured high visibility and continued enthusiasm. Perhaps a million people were involved with one or another aspect of Garvey's nationalist project.

Even after Garvey himself was deported from the United States in 1927 following a conviction for mail fraud, the UNIA continued to operate in numerous urban centers, advocating black repatriation to Africa and a Pan-African identity alongside programs to foster economic independence and racial pride among black people who remained outside the African continent. For a while even the Communist Party tried to appeal to black people along nationalist lines. Beginning in 1928, the party actively advocated for the creation of a separate and self-governing black state carved primarily out of the southern Black Belt—so called for its fertile soil, not its inhabitants—where so many African Americans still lived.

The ideological distinctions that divided nationalism from racial integration, accomodationism from a demand for immediate rights, can be overstated. Du Bois was also a Pan-Africanist, and Garvey cited Washington as a role model. Individual black Americans might simultaneously support the efforts of the NAACP, use the services of the local Colored YWCA, and march in a parade to honor the dream of an all-black nation in Africa. Idealism, race pride, and pragmatism coexisted, sometimes uneasily, in black communities of the early twentieth century.

Beyond political and self-help organizing, the clustering of black communities in urban centers also brought a flourishing social and artistic life. Largely centered in Harlem, New York, and therefore often called the Harlem Renaissance, this explosion of artistic expression transcended a single location. African American writers around the country suddenly found broader audiences for their work, sometimes through the aid of white patrons. Black newspapers and journals discussed their work; music clubs and artist salons provided performance spaces in every city with a black community. Poet Countee Cullen, essayist Alain Locke, author Jean Toomer, and novelist and poet Claude McKay chronicled northern experiences of race; author Zora Neal Hurston offered snapshots of southern black life and celebrated rather than hid the peculiarities of southern black speech. Black painters like Romaire Bearden and William Johnson explored African motifs and celebrated the black body; musicians experimented with the new musical form of jazz. Some black artists tempered any political critique in order to appeal to white audiences, but others took advantage of their newfound acceptance to make political points. "If we must die," penned McKay reflecting on white mob violence, "let us nobly die. . . . /Pressed to the wall/ Dying/But fighting back!"[4]

African Americans' lives remained hard through the early twentieth century, constrained by poverty, discrimination, racism, and their results. Still, by the 1920s there seemed to be some reason for optimism. The numbers of economically, politically, and artistically successful African Americans had grown. Legal and political victories had begun to chip away at the worst abuses. Black workers made inroads into new industries and urban black communities grew in both size and political muscle. But much of this positive momentum would not continue. Employment rates, particularly among the unskilled, both black and white, began to decline during the second half of the decade. Then, in October 1929 the stock market crashed, speeding a collapse in manufacturing that falling employment rates had already signaled. The Great Depression had arrived.

Notes

1. W. E. B. Du Bois, *The Souls of Black Folk*, 2nd ed. (Chicago: 1903), 181.

2. Mary Church Terrell, "First Presidential Address to the NACW," in Beverly Jones, *Quest for Equality: The Life and Writings of Mary Eliza Church Terrell, 1863–1954* (Brooklyn, NY: Carlson Publishing, 1990), 136.

3. "Returning Soldiers," Editorial, *Crisis* 18, no.1 (May 1919): 14.

4. Claude McKay, "If We Must Die," *Liberator* 2 (July 1919): 21. Reprinted in McKay, *Harlem Shadows: The Poems of Claude McKay* (New York: Harcourt Brace & Co., 1922), 53.

~

CHAPTER TWO

Last Hired, First Fired: Working through the Great Depression

The Great Depression devastated the economy. Factories, stores, banks, mills, and business firms collapsed. Others radically cut their workforce. Three million people could not find jobs in January 1930, according to the American Federation of Labor. That figure rose to more than 13.5 million three years later. Wages had fallen to roughly 60 percent of their pre-Depression level. Declining demand followed the decline in earnings, speeding the downward spiral. For farmers, the situation was worsened further by competition from foreign growers and by terrible droughts in 1930 and 1931. The result of these economic contractions was rapidly falling prices, which brought disaster to both the industrial and the farm markets.

The economic crisis affected everyone, rural and urban, skilled and unskilled, black and white. The federal government in 1930 estimated that 17 percent of the white population and 38 percent of the black population could not support themselves without assistance. Those figures soon worsened. African Americans were particularly hard hit, as white men took jobs formerly held by black men, and white women took the jobs of black women. A large proportion of the lucky few black Americans who had earlier managed to finance their own businesses or buy their own homes lost them.

Wages of those still employed plummeted, and professional workers found themselves underemployed or unable to collect fees from their clients. Farm workers struggled to stay on the land or took to the road in hopes of finding work elsewhere. Black workers faced greater competition for even the worst jobs. When successful, organizing by a reinvigorated union movement and by leftist activists eased the worst exploitation, but such efforts were met more often with employer resistance and white violence than with victory. The experiences of black workers differed by region, employment level, gender, origin, and education, but most followed a similarly troubling path. Hunger and homelessness increased; more fell ill. Apartments that housed four might now house eight or ten as needy friends and relatives pooled income and living arrangements just to survive. Charitable organizations were overwhelmed by the need, and the number of children placed in orphanages who still had a living parent skyrocketed. In black communities across the nation, the Great Depression had arrived in a fury.

For farmers, collapsing prices resulted in tragic irony. It became more expensive to farm and ship produce than it could be sold for. Some farmers poured unsold milk onto the ground rather than compounding their losses by shipping it to market, or slaughtered sheep they could no longer afford to feed. Even high yields of cotton or corn brought little easing of debts because prices per bushel had declined so precipitously. Cotton, which had sold for eighteen cents a pound in 1929, had fallen to six cents a pound four years later.

For a variety of reasons, including discrimination and the relative levels of debt, the impact was greater on black farmers than white. After a single year of the Depression, the number of black farm owners had already fallen 5 percent and their total acreage by almost 10 percent. The value of their land had declined by more than a third. By the close of the Depression decade the number of black farmers who owned or managed their own farms had dropped from a quarter of all black agricultural workers to less than 15 percent, even as the proportion of white farm owners and managers rose to almost half of all white farmers.

For those laboring on the land of others, wages fell sharply. In 1931 in Sumter County, South Carolina, farm wages averaged twenty-five cents a day. In nearby Clarendon County, farm workers earned fifteen cents. Sometimes these payments were made in credit redeemable only at the plantation store. A 1934 study found that those families forced to borrow money in order to make ends meet paid local interest rates as high as 37 percent. As a result, sharecroppers and tenants of both races sunk even deeper into debt. The impact of that decline in farm earnings was greater on black professionals and business owners who relied on their patronage than on those businesses serving white communities. Many local shop owners were forced to close. Professionals, including lawyers, doctors, and nurses, might have to accept payment in food or labor if they received anything at all. Congregations could no longer support their ministers.

The Mayberry family, North Carolina sharecroppers, had little to their name in 1933. Here they pose for the Resettlement Administration photographer in front of their home, a rundown house with cracks in the walls and a stone for the front steps. Mayberry family, Iredell Co., N.C., 1933. Courtesy of the Franklin D. Roosevelt Library Digital Archives.

Even excluding families so poor they required government relief, southern black farm families earned less money than white. In fact not only did white Georgia sharecroppers earn more than black sharecroppers, they earned more than black farm owners. In North Carolina, while black farm owners earned slightly more than white sharecroppers in their state, they lagged well behind white farm owners (see table 2.1).

Such disparities existed across the South. In his research for a Depression-era study of black Americans, Thomas Woofter discovered that in the 600

Table 2.1. Average Annual Earnings of Farm Families by Race, 1936

State	Black	White
Georgia		
Sharecroppers	$422	$583
Owners	$533	$794
North Carolina		
Sharecroppers	$803	$1,036
Owners	$1,053	$1,590

southern counties he studied, black cotton sharecroppers netted an annual income of $295, compared to $417 for white sharecroppers. Black wage farmers working in cotton earned an average of $175 a year, Woofter found, compared with $232 for whites.

Not surprisingly, such low earnings and high debt meant that these families lived in horrifying conditions. When desperation led to crime—or when railroaded into false arrests and convictions—southern black convicts found themselves in even worse straits, forced to labor on harsh chain gangs in prisons like the notorious Parchman Penitentiary in Mississippi. If prison officials did not themselves put inmates to work, local white landowners seeking cheap labor paid convicts' fines and then compelled their labor as repayment, in a system known as convict leasing.

Many agricultural workers were forced off the land entirely. Landlords who rented out their land cut back on production by expelling tenant farmers. Where whites tenanted or sharecropped alongside blacks, the latter lost their place sooner. Those few who owned their own land struggled to hold onto it as earnings plummeted. A growing number fell delinquent in their taxes during the Depression years; in response authorities either placed liens on their property or seized the land outright. Even in towns like Promised Land, a South Carolina Piedmont community of black-owned farms, the value of personal property, low to begin with, declined by one-third in the course of the decade. It fell by half for those without land. Meanwhile, natural disasters brought their own perils. Drought, dust storms, and poor soil conservation practices led to substantial loss of farmable land in the Dust Bowl. The continued spread of the cotton-destroying boll weevil and flooding in the Mississippi Delta, Louisiana, North Carolina, and Texas left thousands more without land to till.

Close to 100,000 sharecroppers lost their livelihood. They and thousands of other southern black agricultural workers, along with family or friends, joined the exodus of migrants searching for a better life. Some sought farm work elsewhere, but most, whether moving North or remaining in the South, headed toward rapidly expanding urban areas. There they pressed into already crowded black neighborhoods, deepening the poverty and hardship there and competing with residents for the limited jobs available. By the end of the Depression one-third of southern African Americans and almost two-thirds of the national black population lived and worked in cities. Yet while urban areas did offer greater job prospects, wages and opportunities there had also declined. Southern mills and factories laid off thousands of workers and paid many of the remaining workers wages lower than they needed to live. Memphis sawmills offered work at seven cents an hour. Those shelling nuts received six cents a pound, or a maximum of four dollars a week. Riverboat workers there earned eight cents an hour for eighteen-hour days.

African Americans hovered at the bleakest end of the southern economy. Legal segregation and overt discrimination continued to exact high costs, and those who remained at work continued to find their lives degrading, constrained, and dangerous. They were well aware that only the lowest jobs were available to them, but now they were often last in line even there. In South Carolina, where African Americans constituted almost half of the population, whites outnumbered blacks four to one in mills and factories. Across the South, groups of armed white workers threatened and intimidated employers who hired African Americans, arguing that they must hire the white unemployed first. The June 1931 *Monthly Labor Review* reported that replacing black workers with whites was a common practice. In Mobile, Alabama, Dry Dock and Shipbuilding Company brought in white migrants to fill jobs, and it even employed some white women in traditionally male fields, rather than employ local black workers. As Hilton Butler wrote in *The Nation*, "Dust had been blown from the shotgun, the whip, and the noose, and Ku Klux practices were being resumed in the certainty that dead men not only tell no tales but create vacancies."[1] Even the usually cautious Commission on Interracial Cooperation concluded that lynching had become a tool of economic as well as political exclusion.

Skilled black workers in the South lost much of the tenuous foothold they had gained in earlier decades. In 1930 only approximately 100,000 black men, 3 to 4 percent of all southern black male workers, held skilled positions. Within six years that tiny number had fallen to under 30,000. Along the South Atlantic coast, only black painters and cement finishers expanded in number by the end of the decade. In every other major field of skilled work, both the number and proportion of black workers declined. Tradespeople and professionals employed within the black community, from hairdressers to store owners, watched their client base wither. Thousands lost their businesses entirely. Even physicians and members of the clergy found themselves seeking other employment. In the first six years of the Depression, almost 500 black businesses failed in New Orleans. By 1936 a fifth of all the storefronts in Norfolk, Virginia's black business district were vacant.

As a result, black unemployment rates skyrocketed in the Depression years. Black southern urban unemployment increased from one-third to one-half between 1931 and 1932. In some places, rates ran even higher. In Memphis, African Americans made up just over a third of the total population, but 75 percent of the unemployed. In Atlanta, almost 70 percent of black workers had no jobs in 1934. The proportion of black families in Norfolk applying for aid topped 80 percent. In every case, black unemployment rates in southern cities and towns doubled or even tripled those of whites.

Underemployment, which plagued workers of every race and skill level as companies fought desperately to stem their losses, also hit black workers harder than whites. Black workers usually found their hours cut sooner and more dramatically. Meanwhile, their history of lower pay meant they had less to cushion them during these hard times. In Norfolk, even those families with at least one member employed in a nondomestic job struggled; more than a third reported they were in debt. Some had lost the homes they had worked so hard to purchase. Of those with any savings at home or in bank accounts, none had accumulated more than fifty dollars.

Certainly those with jobs fared better than those with none, but the earnings of black workers in southern cities continued to lag well behind whites. In Atlanta, the median annual income for black families in 1936 came to only about a third of that of white families. The situation was similar in Mobile, where black families fared substantially worse than whites (see table 2.2). These discrepancies remained whether comparing households with one parent or with two. In fact black families with two parents, even those of skilled workers, earned significantly less than white families with only one parent present.

A White House conference on children described this pattern across the South. Overall in 1936, white families in southern cities earned three times what black families did. More than half of all southern urban black families reported annual incomes of $750 or less that year, compared with about 12 percent of white families. On the other end of the earnings spectrum, more than a quarter of whites but fewer than 2 percent of blacks earned more than $2,500. It is hard to imagine families surviving on so little especially when, as the White House report reminded its readers, crowded and segregated black families usually paid more for housing than did white. In every city the decline in earnings from before the Depression far surpassed the drop in the cost of living, making it even harder to make ends meet than before.

Table 2.2. Median Family Income by Race and Family Status in Mobile and Atlanta

City	Two-parent Families	Single-parent Families
Mobile		
African American	$481	$301
White	$1,419	$784
Atlanta		
African American	$632	$332
White	$1,876	$940

Economic opportunities were somewhat better in northern and western cities. There, discrimination was less overt and not enshrined in the law, and a history of local black activism meant that there were already mechanisms in place to challenge the worst outrages. In 1936 northern urban black family income came to almost two-thirds of white, well above the southern ratio. Not surprisingly, leaving the South proved an attractive option. By 1940 approximately 1.75 million black residents had moved to northern and western cities.

Nevertheless, like their southern counterparts, these urban black workers still suffered from multiple handicaps when it came to keeping their jobs during the Depression. The more industrialized North experienced higher levels of unemployment, given the collapse in production. Within each industry, unskilled labor was hit the hardest, the job category reported by the vast majority of black workers. But as in the South, at every skill level, northern black workers suffered more than whites, for reasons of past as well as present discrimination. When northern employers allocated cutbacks and layoffs fairly, length of time on the job largely determined workers' hours and positions. Even black people who had lived in the region for many years lacked seniority, given employers' long-standing preference for white workers. Therefore, earlier patterns of discrimination ensured that even in cases of equitable cutbacks, most black workers lost their jobs sooner than whites. A greater proportion of skilled black men in the North than in the South reported themselves as holding semiskilled or unskilled jobs or unemployed, and a substantial number of those who still held skilled positions worked in government-funded New Deal programs.

More often than not, however, even in the North, employers did not allocate layoffs and cutbacks fairly, and racism continued to affect employment patterns. Being white doubled one's chances of finding work. The figures varied by city, skill level, and gender, but the pattern of higher black unemployment held. In 1932 approximately 25 percent of all white workers in the urban North reported themselves unable to find work. For black workers the figures ran significantly higher throughout the decade. In Pittsburgh and Chicago, half reported they had no work. In Philadelphia and Detroit, black unemployment approached 60 percent. In each case these figures were substantially higher than those for whites. As late as 1940, as the Depression began to ease, almost twice as many northern black men as white reported themselves unemployed. African Americans lamented that they were consistently "last hired, first fired" when employers could have their pick of workers. And many of these men and women remained unemployed for years. Of those unable to find work in 1940, 20 percent of African

Americans, but only 7 percent of whites, reported that they had not been able to find work for four years or more.

As in the South, northern unemployment and underemployment also had a greater impact on black lives because of their long-standing poverty and therefore relatively lower level of savings. In one Philadelphia study, only half of the black families between 1930 and 1932 had any savings at all. Investigators estimated that, on average, among those with savings and some credit, white unemployed families could continue for approximately eight months at their regular living standard, but black families could do so for only six weeks. In fact, unemployed white families reported cutting back their spending by 50 percent and black families by 75 percent. Because black workers found it harder to make ends meet even when employed, they felt the consequences of unemployment more quickly and dramatically.

Most African American workers who did succeed in obtaining or keeping their jobs labored in unskilled and service fields, regardless of their actual skills. In the Middle Atlantic and North Central states, the areas of greatest industrial activity, fewer than 40 percent of male skilled workers in 1936 reported holding jobs at their skill level. In New York City, the Urban League and the New York State Employment Service reported that although a quarter of black job seekers in New York City qualified for skilled or white-collar work, almost 90 percent of the jobs available to black workers were in unskilled fields.

Such tremendous economic pressures made northern black earnings for both professionals and blue-collar workers fall almost as dramatically as those of their southern counterparts. Part of that decline was the result of a general decline in wages; more reflected the large number who worked at jobs below their training. But the greatest burden once again fell on the poor. The incomes of unskilled laborers, the vast majority of the black working population, declined to roughly a third of what they had been before the Depression.

As a result, many black families in the North as well as the South were forced to get by on incomes well under what federal and local agencies considered a minimum standard of living. In Chicago, the Works Progress Administration (WPA) estimated in mid-decade that for a married laborer with two children to meet rental, food, and clothing costs, with no additional expenditures—what it termed an "emergency budget"—required $973 a year. More than 40 percent of Chicago's black families lived at or below this level. Among those with jobs in industry or domestic service, two-thirds earned less.

Emergency budgets could not sustain a family for long. The WPA therefore also calculated what it termed a "maintenance budget," or enough money to survive without major hardship for a longer period. A 1935 survey of Harlem found that while average family earnings there did exceed the WPA's emergency budget for New York, they fell below its maintenance budget. White families in New York, by contrast, earned more than enough to meet maintenance levels. At the same time, more black families were among the poorest: nearly a quarter of black families who did not receive relief survived on less than the minimum estimated emergency budget in the city. Indeed, African Americans as a whole in New York fared worse than poor whites there: one study found that even white families living in New York's most run-down tenement houses had higher median household incomes than did black families living in Harlem.

These racial disparities were visible at every level and in every region. In Chicago in 1936, more than twice as many black families as white earned less than $500. On the other extreme, only a tiny percentage of black families, but almost a third of whites, earned more than $2,000. These disparities remained regardless of family structure or occupational level. The average black laborer in New York working all year long earned what white laborers could earn in eight months. Black male clerical workers' salaries averaged only three-quarters those of white male clerical workers.

Thus, many skilled and educated black workers saw their opportunities for good jobs decline, finding themselves working in those unskilled or service jobs usually relegated to African Americans. But now, North or South, there were no longer any purely "black" occupations. During the Depression, there were no jobs white workers refused to do. This meant even greater employment insecurity; African Americans could no longer even count on access to the worst jobs. White men cleaned streets and collected garbage, jobs formerly reserved for black workers. The Atlanta School of Social Work reported in 1933 that white men in that city had been taking jobs as garbage men, waiters, bellhops, elevator operators, delivery boys, and chauffeurs—jobs that paid little but had, as a result, offered reliable employment for African Americans in the past. Other studies found the same patterns of white workers replacing black all over the country. In Seattle, when struggling companies and families cut back on hiring, black stewards and hotel, railroad, and domestic workers lost their jobs. Those who were able to keep their jobs saw their wages cut dramatically. As a result, the number of black families on relief in that city quadrupled just between 1930 and 1931. These patterns held everywhere.

Black women faced similar job pressures as men. Married or single, they continued to work far more frequently than white women. The numbers of employed black married women remained at just over a third across the decade, more than three times the rate of native-born whites. While these working black women generally held different jobs from black men, they too remained at the bottom of their occupational ladder. The number of black women in manufacturing dropped by a third, for example; most of these women ended up in domestic work. But generally when black women lost their jobs, they lost them to white women rather than to men. While white men would now accept jobs previously left for black men, few willingly crossed gender boundaries to accept jobs more commonly associated with women, although white women were known to replace black men in service jobs, such as waiting tables.

Almost half of all employed black women held jobs as servants or domestic workers, positions that remained firmly in the category of women's work. There were suddenly many more white laundry workers or those employed in tailoring and sewing than before the Depression, for example, but they were still largely female. In Norfolk, white women threatened to fire their black domestic workers in favor of needy white women and later, a number of sewing rooms funded by the government-run WPA replaced black women with white. In neither case did anyone propose hiring men. The reverse was true as well. Distinct gender roles in employment were widely accepted in this era for both women and men. When the Birmingham WPA assigned black women heavy construction jobs, the local NAACP protested that such work was inappropriate.

Ironically, in some cases the divided labor market proved advantageous to working women, white or black. Because the Depression affected traditionally male fields of manufacturing and construction most severely, some traditional female jobs like teaching and nursing proved more secure. The persistence of gender divisions, therefore, meant that both white and black women fared a bit better in terms of finding employment than their male counterparts. On the other hand, the desperation of these women meant wages could drop to almost nothing, and employers could still find women willing to take those jobs. In 1935 Marvel Cooke and Ella Baker published an exposé of the exploitation of domestic workers in the NAACP's *Crisis* magazine. The conditions were so dreadful they titled their piece "The Bronx Slave Market." They described black women seeking domestic work in New York who stood on street corners while white housewives bartered for the lowest possible wages. Cheating by employers was also common, but these women had no recourse. They had to feed their families, even on the fifteen or twenty cents an hour they received. Across the city, black domestics reported earning between $6 and $10 dollars a week, a dramatic drop from even the low $15 they averaged in the 1920s. Domestic wages were similarly dreadful in every city studied. Well over half of Birmingham's black domestic workers earned less than $200 for an entire year of work.

Women also earned less than men for work at the same occupations. New York women in laundry work, all races combined, earned $13 per week, a dollar less than men received. Black women earned less than $9 for the same work. Among unskilled workers, black women earned roughly half as much as black men. Black women doing clerical work earned only about two-thirds of what their male counterparts did. Similar disparities appeared at all employment levels and in all regions of the country. Racial lines of employment blurred in the desperate rush to the bottom, but, for both good and ill, gender lines held fast. As black women had noted for years, race and gender compelled them to carry a double burden.

Greater black unemployment and underemployment also meant that across the nation more black teens than white teens were compelled to work. Despite the National Youth Administration and other government-aid programs for young people, almost 40 percent of nonwhite males and 18 percent of females between fourteen and nineteen years old held jobs in 1940, compared to a quarter of white. For young women, the proportions were 18 percent for nonwhites and 13 percent for whites. Because employment usually meant an end to education, the racial disparities in youth employment had implications for the future as well. More years in school yielded better employment and higher earnings later; in that way the greater black poverty in the Depression era that compelled young people to work also meant greater black poverty in the next generation.

The Depression was hardly kinder to the tiny black middle class. In 1939 there were fewer than 30,000 black-owned businesses in the entire United States. Sales had declined almost 30 percent since 1929. With less capital and more dependent on an impoverished clientele, black businesses failed more often and more quickly than those owned by whites. A single white insurance company held more African American policies than all the black insurance companies combined. Some black businesses, like the Atlanta Life Insurance Company and the North Carolina Mutual Life Insurance Company, survived the Depression; a few even prospered. But for the vast majority in both North and South, the hard-won gains from the past twenty years were lost in the Depression decade. This included even large institutions like Binga State Bank of Chicago, black-owned and black-run since 1908, with over $1.5 million in deposits. Of the 134 black banks established before the Great Depression, only 12 remained in 1936. Urban black businesses collapsed at an alarming rate and black real estate developers were forced to sell their buildings to white absentee owners. Even in Harlem, where the number of black businesses actually increased, profits declined. Many did not have a single paid employee. As elsewhere, a majority of its black-owned real estate turned over to white hands.

Nor did many African Americans make it to professional ranks during the Depression decade. As late as 1940 only 2 percent of all doctors in the United States were black—a 10 percent decline from 1930. Black nurses constituted less than 2 percent of all nurses. Among lawyers, less than 1 percent were African American. All in all, just under 3 percent of employed black men and just under 5 percent of black women held professional jobs in 1940. White rates were three times as high.

In the North as well as in the South, the earnings of these and other professionals plummeted during the Depression as their clients' ability to pay for their services declined. In New York, black professionals suffered a one-third drop in income from pre-Depression figures, to $1,440. Black female professionals earned even less. By contrast, white professionals there earned more than twice as much. Everywhere, black physicians, lawyers, writers, social workers, and other highly trained individuals found themselves compelled to find alternative employment or apply for government help. The same was true for many black clergy, who suffered alongside their congregations. Journalist George Schuyler's melodramatic observation about railway baggage handlers seemed apt through the Depression decade: "Turn a machine gun on a crowd of red caps . . . and you would slaughter a score of Bachelors of Arts, Doctors of Law, Doctors of Medicine, Doctors of Dental Surgery."[2]

Black employment opportunities in white-collar areas did expand in the government sector, as New Deal programs increased the number of public jobs. Because most of these new agencies had nondiscrimination provisions, black workers at all levels of skill had a better chance to obtain these jobs than those in the private sector where racial discrimination remained pervasive. Certainly many government programs disregarded nondiscrimination rules, and elsewhere discriminatory labor unions excluded potential black workers. But other government agencies engaged large numbers of black workers, including 18,000 employed by the U.S. Postal Service alone. Although most black employees still worked in the same menial jobs they found in private employment, many government programs—particularly in northern and western cities—also hired black skilled, clerical, and professional workers. That group included a substantial number of black social workers, teachers, nurses, office managers, architects, engineers, and administrators. Fully a fifth of all those working in skilled jobs held them thanks to government work. New Deal programs had a tremendous impact on black employment levels and occupational patterns.

One promising development for workers was the growth of trade unions. Both New Deal legislation and economic hardship gave unionism a boost. In 1932 section 7A of the National Industrial Recovery Act (NIRA) for the first time guaranteed workers the right to organize unions. In 1935, after the Supreme Court declared the NIRA unconstitutional, Congress passed the Wagner National Labor Relations Act, which extended 7A's scope. It prohibited company (employer-created) unions, protected organizing workers against employer retaliation, and required good faith negotiations between worker representatives and employers.

All types of unions benefited from New Deal labor legislation. Craft unions, those organized around specific and hard-to-obtain skills, had begun organizing in the nineteenth century, and their successes relied on limiting the number of workers available to perform the tasks. The Brotherhood of Locomotive Firemen and Enginemen, for example, managed to keep wages relatively high because a strike would cripple the industry. Employers could not find enough skilled and trained strikebreakers to do what they needed.

The New Deal labor laws solidified the base of craft unions but did not have much impact on black employment, since these unions continued to restrict the jobs they controlled to white workers. By 1928, for example, the railroad unions had managed to bar black firemen, brakemen, yardmen, and trainmen from the field entirely, despite the opposition not only of the African American workers but of the railroads themselves. As of 1935, more than twenty craft unions still explicitly barred nonwhite members. Many others segregated black members, denied them voting rights, or used more informal mechanisms of exclusion. As a result, black union membership remained low, estimated at somewhere between 50,000 and 100,000.

Industrial unions, by contrast, organized largely by and for unskilled and semiskilled workers, could not employ such exclusionary tactics. If laundry or construction workers walked off the job in protest, employers could easily find thousands of desperate unemployed people eager to take their place. Before the New Deal, unskilled and semiskilled workers faced almost insurmountable odds against successful organizing. Now, newly protected by federal labor legislation and spurred to greater efforts by the economic desperation, a group of union organizers set out to aid these industrial and unskilled workers they had largely neglected before. Most worked through a Committee on Industrial Organizing established in 1935 within the American Federation of Labor. Two years after it was founded, the committee had more members than the rest of the AFL. In 1938 the two separated and the committee became the Congress of Industrial Organizations (CIO).

Since it was impossible to limit the number of people capable of doing the work, industrial union organizers sought instead to engage all possible workers in the struggle for union recognition. When racist whites excluded black workers, organizers pointed out, employers hired the latter as strikebreakers. Only by offering union membership and benefits to all, regardless of race, could unskilled and industrial unions succeed. Thus most such unions, or at least their leadership, were devotedly antiracist and actively sought to recruit African American workers along with whites. If African Americans did not become union brothers and sisters, they might become scabs. This breadth of outreach provided much of the momentum behind the great West Coast Waterfront Strike (also known as the Longshoremen's Strike) of 1934, an eighty-three-day strike that shut down docks on the West Coast. The first general strike in U.S. history, it included sailors, cooks, stewards, and dock workers, affecting more than 2,000 black and white workers in Seattle alone.

Among these organizers were many Socialists and Communists, drawn to this unionizing movement out of a political conviction that the working class was the victim of an exploitative capitalist system. The harsh realities of the Depression made their arguments even more convincing. Only unity among all workers could overthrow the tyranny of their bosses, they insisted, and bring substantive economic change. They considered racism a tool for the wealthy to divide workers and dilute their power. Thus their politics as well as realities of organizing the unskilled convinced them to welcome black workers. As black Communist leader James Ford argued, the benefits worked in both directions. Unionizing helped desperate, unemployed black workers while including black members improved the chances for successful organizing. "The struggle for Negro freedom and Negro rights depends upon the organization of the masses to struggle for their daily immediate needs, better wages, unemployment and social insurance, civil rights and equal rights," he insisted.[3] To better achieve these goals, the Communist Party announced its Popular Front strategy of working with liberal groups when doing so advanced common goals. Communists, therefore, embraced all progressive union activists as coalition partners in organizing efforts.

A few unions had already begun organizing around the principles that interracial unions advanced the interests of all workers. The United Mineworkers Union, for example, was interracial from its inception in 1890. Because African Americans already worked in mining, and because mining involved so many different types of tasks, any union had to incorporate all workers to avoid strikebreaking. Black and white organizers built the union together. The International Ladies Garment Workers' Union, one of the most famous examples of an interracial industrial union, began this inclusive style of organizing in the early twentieth century. But more, like the Dockworkers and United Auto Workers, saw their first broad organizing successes during the Depression, as new black as well as white members joined their ranks.

Inspired by these ideas, two Socialist activists, Don West and Myles Horton, established the Highlander Folk School in Monteagle, Tennessee, in 1932. Designed as a cooperative center for developing effective organizing strategies and an open forum for leftist discussions, Highlander centered its training around the conviction that workers become empowered by making decisions for themselves. In the Depression years, the Folk School trained hundreds of labor activists; within a decade Highlander shifted its focus to civil rights and became a strategy and training center for that movement as well.

Many African Americans, recognizing both the potential of union organizing and the pervasive racism of existing unions, organized or reinvigorated their own unionizing projects, as did Frank Crosswaith with the Negro Labor Committee. Crosswaith, a Socialist, worked with local unions in New York City to integrate their ranks and with local black workers to convince them of the importance of unionizing. A. Philip Randolph's Brotherhood of Sleeping Car Porters and Maids, which gained formal recognition from the Pullman Company only in 1937, also aided other workers' efforts. From Memphis to San Francisco, union struggles coincided with black struggles for decent jobs at fair wages.

The CIO and its allies organized across the country, in the South as well as the North and West, reaching out to black workers who unloaded cargo on the docks, farmed the land, mined for coal, or worked in laundries, textile or automobile factories, steel mills, or packing houses. Black and white female nut pickers in St. Louis struck for better pay in 1933 and the owners raised wages and recognized the Food Workers Industrial Union. In Chicago, black and white women struck at a clothing factory, winning higher wages and equal pay for black and white workers. The International Longshore and Warehouse Union, under the leadership of Harry Bridges, fought for integration of the docks at West Coast ports; the West Coast Waterfront Strike was part of this effort. The Steel Workers Organizing Committee (SWOC), set up in 1936, worked with the NAACP, National Urban League, and National Negro Congress to recruit black members. SWOC held integrated meetings and appointed African Americans to union office in many of its locals, in the South as well the North. Even the International Association of Machinists, an all-white craft union, expanded its reach in 1936 to include semiskilled and unskilled workers, in this one stroke integrating its membership.

Unionizing clearly benefited African Americans who had, for so long, labored longer hours at harder jobs for less pay than their white coworkers. Although at first white workers perceived black involvement as a threat to their jobs, the hard-fought pay increases and shorter work hours won by SWOC and others demonstrated the benefits that interracial unions offered whites as well. Their successes also demonstrated that black cooperation was crucial in establishing and sustaining these unions, so these organizing efforts built on one another. In 1939 female tobacco workers struck in Richmond and formed the Tobacco Workers Organizing Committee. By 1943 they had compelled even the large R. J. Reynolds Company to negotiate with them. The United Auto Workers, whose past record on race had not been positive, overcame tremendous black distrust to win a union contract at Ford in 1941 only after working with black organizations, hiring racially progressive organizers, clamping down on informal racist practices, and becoming more outspoken on civil rights issues. Interestingly, a number of local African American leaders supported Ford against the strikers. But a year or so later when the CIO defended the right of black workers to obtain their share of defense jobs, even these conservative leaders came around. As a result of such efforts, approximately 200,000 black workers held membership in a union by 1940.

As Crosswaith, Randolph, and others had promised, incorporating black workers in organizing drives proved mutually beneficial. Unionizing helped black workers, and black workers helped build unions. Indeed, as many scholars have argued, not only did organizing in the New Deal and war years improve conditions for black workers within the union movement, black union activists advanced liberal democracy, social justice, and the power of organized labor in the nation as a whole. In so many examples, from interracial union organizing in Memphis to the story of the Winston-Salem chapter of the Food, Tobacco, Agricultural and Allied Workers of America or the longshoremen and seamen on both coasts, black and white union members forged an interracial framework for challenging the control of white conservative businessmen and politicians. Through integrated union meetings, classes on labor history, education programs, sports and music clubs, these and other union locals offered new possibilities for interracial organizing around issues of democracy and workers' rights. Working together, black and white workers strengthened the power they held over their working conditions and their earnings. Furthermore, they helped pioneer tactics that other progressive struggles would use, from the civil rights and feminist movements to those for disability rights and against South African apartheid.

Certainly, significant barriers to organizing black workers remained. Virtually every effort to unionize brought resistance, even violence, from powerful interests. Police beat, arrested, and even on occasion shot protesters and organizers, often assisted by other angry whites. A 1931 strike of New Orleans dockworkers resulted in more than a hundred arrests, most of them of black workers. The Georgia Klan, unhappy at the advancement of black textile workers as a result of a union drive, responded with a violent anti-CIO campaign in 1939. Even in the North and West demonstrators faced intimidation. Local police attacked workers at a Seattle demonstration and then arrested the protest speakers for inciting riot.

That Communists led many of these organizing projects intensified the threat of violence even further. Many linked Communists and Socialists with the authoritarian Soviet Union. Closer to home, they feared that these leftists' anticapitalist stance threatened business. Most southern whites interpreted the Communists' interracial union organizing as a Soviet plot to destroy the United States by undermining traditional race relations. Communist agitators, they were convinced, stirred up otherwise contented black Americans to demand an equality they did not deserve and—even worse—sought to bring down the white race by granting black men ready access to white women. Such inflammatory rhetoric, so useful in preserving economic advantages for the white middle and upper classes, brought anti-union violence to new heights.

African American Hosea Hudson became active in Communist Party organizing around labor issues in and around Birmingham beginning in 1930. At mass meetings public speakers like Hudson laid out the harsh conditions facing the unemployed and placed the blame on the capitalist system and the local bosses who propelled it. These speakers argued that segregation, lynching, poor wages, unemployment, and union busting all worked together to weaken the poor and enrich the employers. The only productive response, they insisted, was racial unity between black and white workers who together could smash the system. Police routinely broke up these public meetings, often violently. A 1930 meeting in Birmingham led to the firebombing of that speaker's home. In 1933 police tried to shut down a demonstration there attended by approximately 3,000 people, many of whom were African American. When demonstrators refused to yield, the police attacked. Hudson encountered violence in every city and town in which he tried to organize.

In Atlanta in 1930, police used a slave statute to arrest two black men, two white men, and two white women for "attempting to incite insurrection."

Their crime: holding an integrated protest against unemployment and in support of striking textile workers. Although the "Atlanta Six" never went to trial, the charges against them were not formally dismissed until 1939. African American Communist Angelo Herndon was even less fortunate. In 1932 he led an integrated unemployment protest in Atlanta. Police arrested him for violating the same slave statute and beat him. When he was found guilty and sentenced to eighteen to twenty years on a chain gang, he became a cause célèbre for the Communist Party. For five years the party marshaled thousands of prominent men and women and hundreds of thousands of rank-and-file supporters to demand Herndon's freedom. As part of its Popular Front strategy the party also collaborated with the black press, the NAACP, ACLU, Central Conference of American Rabbis, Brotherhood of Sleeping Car Porters, League for Industrial Democracy, and other non-Communist groups. Finally, in 1937, the Supreme Court reversed Herndon's conviction, ruling that his rights under the Fourteenth Amendment had been violated.

These harsh reprisals against Communist and Socialist organizing made it exceedingly difficult to recruit new members or to get support from liberal organizations for the party's programs. Only one white local group came out in support of the Atlanta Six, the Socialist-based Workmen's Circle. Nevertheless, as the Herndon case and the unionizing campaigns of mine, tobacco, and other workers reveal, a number of these struggles succeeded. The Textile Workers did unionize in Greenville, South Carolina, despite vicious repression, and Hosea Hudson became one of the first black recording secretaries of the Steelworkers' Union in 1937.

More difficult for black workers to understand was the violent resistance of many white workers and even union members. While industrial unions proved more friendly to black workers than most craft unions, virtually none welcomed them enthusiastically. Racism ran rampant even in the most progressively led unions, as local members and shop stewards continued to favor white workers over black, or to treat African Americans with disdain—or worse. Whites frequently launched protests, work stoppages, or walked off the job when black workers first came onto the dock or shop floor; occasionally there was violence. In such cases white union leaders were forced to choose between integrating workers or maintaining white support for the union struggle. Other unions, like the railroad brotherhoods, continued to hold tenaciously to their white supremacist origins despite the argument that doing so ran against their economic self-interest. As a result, even in the Depression, roughly the same number of African Americans got jobs thru strikebreaking as they did by joining unions, and the NAACP pursued litigation against discriminatory unions into the war years and beyond.

Most of the industrial organizing took place in cities. In the rural South, desperate black farmers and white and black Communists who supported them launched their own organizing campaigns. Seeking both political and economic change, such groups fought for better terms for black and white tenants and sharecroppers, more equitable distribution of aid, and an end to racial discrimination. Some sought to pool agricultural produce in order to raise prices, others to improve farming techniques or increase land ownership by black farmers. The rural South, however, proved even less hospitable to black or interracial organizing, and pervasive racism, virulent anti-Communism, and white violence limited their impact.

African American farmer Ned Cobb worked with the Sharecroppers' Union in Alabama, organized with Communist Party support in 1931. Struggling for a decent life, Cobb understood the relationship between his poverty and southern racism. "Ever since I been in God's world, I've never had no rights, no voice in nothin that the white man didn't want me to have—even been cut out of education, book learnin, been deprived of that."[4] White landowners and storekeepers consistently cheated black farmers and customers with impunity. The results were desperate. "Conditions has been outrageous every way that you can think against the colored race of people." Hearing about the Sharecroppers' Union's organizing efforts, he understood it was "somethin unusual," not only because it was "an organization for the poor class of people" but because it was deliberately interracial. White and black organizers encouraged local sharecroppers and tenant farmers to stick together in order to obtain fairer treatment and to defend their rights, supported by the union. As Cobb explained to his neighbors, "The organization would back up and fight your battles with you."[5] Indeed it did. A standoff in Reeltown between the sharecroppers and the deputy sheriff turned bloody. Cobb and other armed local men resisted the sheriff's attempt to seize a man's property. Both sides fired weapons. Three black men died of their wounds and the inability to get medical help; Cobb and several others were arrested and jailed. Lawyers from the party's International Labor Defense (ILD) defended Cobb and the others. After Cobb lost the case, the ILD mounted a number of (ultimately unsuccessful) appeals. In the end, Cobb served thirteen years in prison.

Despite this and other bloody conflicts, the Sharecroppers' Union continued its efforts to organize. By 1933 it reported 5,500 members, mostly African American, and it supported strikes by cotton pickers and other agricultural laborers until its demise in 1939. A 1935 strike by cotton choppers in Alabama brought higher wages in a few counties, but led to arrests and severe beatings by both law enforcement officers and vigilante groups elsewhere in the state, where the strikes collapsed. A pickers' strike later that year resulted in brutal violence, including the beating of dozens of men and women not involved in the union and the killing of at least six.

Similar experiences faced those who joined the Southern Tenant Farmers' Union (STFU), which began organizing in 1934 in Arkansas with the help of Socialist activists. Like the Sharecroppers' Union, it encouraged unity among black and white tenants, and its membership was approximately 50 percent African American. Given the reality of southern life, however, the membership of most of the STFU locals were almost exclusively racially separate. Despite a number of successes in dealings with landowners, including several effective cotton-picker strikes, and despite a claimed membership of 30,000, the union could bring little improvement to the lives of most farm workers and the vast majority remained mired in desperation. As with the Sharecroppers' Union, even the results that successful STFU strikes achieved ended up unraveling as planters reneged on agreements and vigilantes systematically beat and killed those who had been active in the campaigns. The STFU's political outreach, however, was more successful. With the help of the NAACP and Socialist and Communist leaders, the union gained coverage in progressive national journals like the *New Masses*, *The Nation*, *New Republic*, *Opportunity*, *Crisis*, and even *Time* magazine. The resulting public exposure of the exploitative labor and living conditions facing sharecroppers and tenant farmers, and the debilitating levels of illiteracy and disease, prompted some federal intervention to protect these most desperate workers.

The experiences of Hudson, Cobb, and so many others suggest how difficult such organizing proved to be. The willingness of so many black men to stand up to white authority, despite the evident danger, is a testament to the farmers' anger and desperation as well as to their extraordinary courage. Too few citizens, black or white, were willing to risk their jobs, or possibly their lives, for advances that seemed impossible. Some therefore consider such organizing efforts a failure. Nevertheless, these struggles helped build important bridges among progressive communities and tested organizing strategies. Along with other forms of political activism, they formed a base for later civil rights organizing.

The Depression era proved bleak for black workers and their families as they struggled against the dual burdens of racism and economic devastation. Still largely restricted to the worst jobs offering the least pay and mobility, hired last and fired first, African Americans endured dramatic increases in poverty and unemployment and suffered greatly from the ills they produced. The desperation itself, though, did fuel economic and labor protests. While only minimally successful at the time, they provided a repertoire of tactics and rhetoric that would prove crucial to civil rights struggles to come.

Notes

1. Hilton Butler, "Murder for the Job," *The Nation* 137 (July 12, 1933): 44.

2. In Wayne Cooper, ed., *The Passion of Claude McKay: Selected Poetry and Prose, 1912–1948* (New York: Schocken Books, 1973), 255.

3. James Ford, "The Communist's Way Out for the Negro," *Journal of Negro Education* 5, no. 1 (January 1936): 2, 94, 95.

4. Theodore Rosengarten, *All God's Dangers: The Life of Nate Shaw* (New York: Random House, 1984), 314. Shaw was Cobb's pseudonym for the book to protect him and his family.

5. Quotations: Rosengarten, *All God's Dangers*, 314–15, 311, 320, respectively.

CHAPTER THREE

~

Of New Deals and Raw Deals

Franklin D. Roosevelt's New Deal, a potpourri of work, welfare, and development programs, redefined government. Now citizenship entitled all Americans to decent housing and minimally adequate standards of living. Through cash grants and employment programs, the government would "prime the pump" of the economic engine, providing jobs and aid to millions while strengthening the nation's infrastructure.

Among those millions were African Americans, who benefited disproportionately from New Deal programs. Not only were they more often poor than white Americans, but most New Deal agencies explicitly barred racial discrimination. These programs made the difference between food and starvation, allowed children to stay in school and families to keep their homes, and provided new access to skills and jobs. And the visibility of FDR's "Black Cabinet" of African American advisers sent an important and inspirational message to all those looking for evidence that the government supported racial equality.

The New Deal was hardly an unmixed blessing, however. Local officials administered these new federal programs, the same white people who had overseen the patterns of racism and segregation they were now supposed to reject. Despite federal guidelines, most local programs continued to discriminate on racial grounds, especially those in the South. Black farmers lost their land more quickly. African Americans obtained jobs and training far more slowly and received less in economic aid. Public housing officials generally

Hundreds of thousands of children lacked enough food to eat during the Depression. Private charities and government programs offered soup kitchens, free lunch programs, and other meals to hungry youngsters. Here a child is served a school lunch through the Surplus Commodities program, 1936. Courtesy of the Franklin D. Roosevelt Library Digital Archives.

segregated new projects even in the North. New Deal rhetoric was a great deal more egalitarian than the reality.

The fault lay not in the New Deal so much as in the society that produced it. Patterns and practices already established before the Depression rein-forced racial inequality. Scholars term this structural or institutional racism. Segregation into the poorest and most underserved neighborhoods, long-standing exclusion from better-paying jobs and training, educational dispar-ities and other structural impediments to success all meant that even with-out any deliberate racism on the part of New Deal administrators and employers, black opportunities would still have lagged well behind white. While the New Deal proved a turning point for black Americans politically, continued oppression meant that, economically, little changed.

More than a quarter of the American workforce reported themselves un-employed on the eve of the 1932 presidential elections. In black communities, that figure approached 50 percent, higher in many urban industrial centers. Republican president Herbert Hoover intervened economically to provide business, bank, and building loans, and he urged employers not to lay workers off. Still, he held the conservative Republican view that business rather than government should act to improve the economy. As a result, Hoover did little to alleviate the widespread suffering of the unemployed.

Few states and municipalities could offer more. For the most part their aid programs were as undeveloped as the federal government's, and their budgets were decimated by the loss of tax revenue. Some cities, like New Orleans, provided no relief to its citizens at all. It was no surprise, therefore, that overwhelming numbers of working- and middle-class Americans voted for Franklin Roosevelt, the Democratic candidate, despite his vague and conservative-sounding platform. Almost 23 million chose Roosevelt: fewer than 16 million supported Hoover's bid for reelection.

Yet this groundswell of Democratic sentiment did not extend as far into the black community, whose loyalties remained with the party that had won the Civil War and administered Reconstruction. Nor did Roosevelt as a candidate do much to win black allegiance. He preferred to court southern whites, whose votes were critical to his election. Despite overwhelming need, and despite the advocacy of several black leaders including Robert Vann, editor of the *Pittsburgh Courier*, only about a third of African American voters supported Roosevelt. Black majorities supported the Democrats only in a few cities like New York and Kansas City, where local Democratic machines responsive to African American needs had already broken the Republican hold on black votes.

Once in office, Roosevelt began fulfilling his promise of a "New Deal" for the American people. Having no blueprint for restoring economic health, Roosevelt and his advisers instead launched a series of experimental federal programs aimed at helping the needy and reinvigorating the economy. This new alphabet soup of agencies sought to do many things at once: stabilize currency and banking; shore up existing businesses; aid and regulate the housing market; create new jobs for those who could not find any in private industry; and help the unemployed with distributions of clothing, food, and cash payments, called direct relief. Theoretically, all who were poor and all who sought jobs enjoyed equal access to these New Deal programs. As African Americans were well represented among both groups, they were poised to benefit substantially.

Black scholars and civil rights activists worked hard to make sure that African Americans did in fact have equal access to aid. In May 1933 the Rosenwald Fund sponsored a conference on "The Economic Status of the

Negro." Charles Johnson, African American sociologist at Fisk University and former director of research and investigations for the National Urban League, chaired its Findings and Action Committee, which translated the conference's decisions into an action plan. In June the NAACP focused its annual convention on the economic emergency. The next month Joel Spingarn of the NAACP hosted the Second Amenia Conference, which identified steps the new government programs needed to take in order to address the specific challenges facing African Americans.

All sought ways to engage the administration more effectively with black concerns. A delegation led by Edwin Embree, president of the Rosenwald Fund, and Harold Ickes, the white former president of the Chicago NAACP and current secretary of the interior, met with President Roosevelt and pressed him to appoint someone to ensure the fair treatment of African Americans in New Deal programs. The president selected Clark Foreman, a white Georgian, to be adviser to the secretary of the interior on the economic status of Negroes. Foreman in turn hired African American economist Robert Weaver to assist him. When Foreman left for the Works Progress Administration (WPA), Weaver assumed Foreman's position. There being no funds in the federal budget for such work, Foreman's and Weaver's salaries were paid by the Rosenwald Fund.

Constrained by their tiny budget and staff and their lack of institutional clout, their impact was necessarily limited. Still, Foreman and Weaver alerted agency heads to special issues facing African American workers or relief clients, and pushed them to set and enforce nondiscrimination provisions. Foreman also headed an advisory Interdepartmental Group Concerned with Special Problems of Negroes. This group of black and white agency administrators met only a few times, but their concerns were taken up by other coordinating and oversight groups, primarily spearheaded by African Americans. When the National Industrial Recovery Act (NIRA) passed in 1933, for example, Weaver and attorney John Davis set up a watchdog committee they called the Negro Industrial League. The NIRA established the National Recovery Administration (NRA) to stabilize business by setting minimum wages and maximum hours for dozens of industries, issues of obvious concern to black as well as white workers. The league monitored all NRA announcements regarding labor and race, testified at more than a hundred of the code hearings that set standards for each economic sector, and lobbied for equal treatment of black and white workers.

In the autumn of that year, more than twenty civil rights and civic organizations formed a larger coalition, the Joint Committee on National Recovery, to coordinate their separate efforts to address racial inequities. The Negro Industrial League merged with it and John Davis headed the new group. Weaver became its director of research. Still poorly funded, the committee's paid staff consisted of two people, who managed an annual budget of less than $5,000. Unable to do more than monitor government racial practices and issue press releases, the committee nevertheless fought hard to keep the issue of discrimination and civil rights in the public eye. It persuaded the NRA to stand firm on equal pay for black and white workers, for example, despite pleas by southern businessmen for differentials based on race. Although equal pay rules were routinely ignored, their existence itself constituted an important step forward.

This relatively small group of activist white and black administration officials worked hard to challenge entrenched racism. The Public Works Administration (PWA), part of the NIRA, hired workers to build public buildings and other facilities. As one of his first acts as secretary of the interior, Harold Ickes forbade discrimination on any PWA projects. Weaver and Harvard University law professor William Hastie succeeded in inserting a further requirement that every PWA project hire black skilled labor in proportion to their population in the local area.

Additional white allies, including Secretary of Commerce Daniel Roper, Will Alexander, Rexford Tugwell of the Farm Security Administration, and Harry Hopkins, who administered the New Deal's work relief agencies, also appointed African Americans to important posts and challenged segregation in hiring and allocations. Several programs appointed special advisers or even "Negro Divisions" to ensure equity, such as the one headed by political activist Mary McLeod Bethune in the National Youth Administration. Aubrey Williams advised Hopkins on racial matters regarding relief. By 1939 almost every program had at least one "Negro adviser." Other African Americans also held high-ranking administrative posts, like William Hastie, who became assistant solicitor for the Department of the Interior and was appointed a U.S. federal judge in 1937. National Urban League head Eugene Kinckle Jones joined the Department of Commerce. Sociologist Ira DeAugustine Reid took a post in the new Social Security Administration, and welfare and social work activist Lawrence Oxley accepted one in the Labor Department.

Neither these appointments nor the rules prohibiting discrimination could improve conditions, however, if agency administrators did not support racial equality. The NRA was particularly notorious for its refusal to consider the needs of black workers as it determined and implemented farming and industry regulations. Although NRA codes required equal pay for black and white workers at the same jobs, local administrators routinely ignored those provisions, with no repercussions from above. In other cases, employers themselves refused to obey equity rules. In Forrest City, Arkansas, a clothing company required by NRA codes to pay black and white women equally, persisted in paying black workers half of what whites received. After the Joint Committee on Economic Recovery filed a complaint with the NRA in early 1934, the company fired all its black employees and replaced them with whites.

Because the NRA generally accepted local wage and hiring practices, African American workers who kept their jobs continued to face the same discrimination they had before the New Deal. Worse, perhaps, given African American employment patterns, the NRA set very low minimum wages for unskilled work. Agriculture and domestic work were not covered by NRA at all. Frustrated African Americans dubbed the agency "Negro Run Around," "Negroes Robbed Again," or "Negro Removal Agency." Despite the NRA's promise of stable jobs and equitable wages, African Americans were not sorry to see the end of that particular program in 1935 when the Supreme Court declared it an unconstitutional intrusion into private commercial activity.

Even sympathetic white directors could do little when faced with adamant resistance from local whites. Harold Ickes was forced to compromise PWA antidiscrimination requirements in Atlanta, Memphis, and several other southern cities because local administrators simply refused to comply with his directives. Indeed, because virtually all New Deal programs were administered locally, well-intended rules by agency heads in Washington, D.C., were often ignored on the ground. In the South even government employment services were segregated. Black applicants were offered vocational training or employment in only the most menial and poorly paid occupations. Many of those concerned about the plight of African Americans faced two unattractive choices—continue to struggle inside a system that too often failed, or resign in disgust.

President Roosevelt, who promised equality and opportunity for what he termed "the forgotten man," and who was aware of the barriers facing black people, was nevertheless largely unwilling to challenge segregation and discrimination head on. In the "solid South," long-serving Democratic elected officials supported white supremacy as well as the New Deal, and their seniority in Congress meant they controlled important committees. Roosevelt feared that taking on segregation would alienate them, which would in turn undermine his carefully constructed political coalition and jeopardize his legislative priorities. He was not willing to take that risk. As a result, Roosevelt did little in the first years of his presidency to enforce or even encourage civil rights provisions.

The Federal Emergency Relief Administration (FERA) offers a vivid example of rampant racial inequities. In its two years of operation, it spent $4 billion, primarily through the distribution of direct financial relief to the needy. Such payments were routinely more generous to whites, especially in the South. In Jacksonville, Florida, 15,000 black families received 45 percent of the available funds, and 5,000 white families received 55 percent. Houston's black families on relief averaged only three-fourths of what white families received. In Atlanta, although the average white family got almost $33 in relief each month, the average black family was compelled to rely on less than $20. Rural families fared even worse. Black rural families on relief in 1935 received $9 a month; similar white families received $15. Such pay disparities were routine across the South. Officials explained that because black people had lower living standards, they required less money to meet their needs.

Black applicants were also denied relief more often. In Mississippi, with its African American majority, only 9 percent received any relief at all in 1932, compared with 14 percent of whites. Birmingham officials routinely rejected black applicants as "undeserving," despite the fact that many private southern charities and soup kitchens refused to serve African Americans. Even northern cities with substantial black voting populations turned away black applicants for aid more often than white.

Not all of this was due to overt racism. Some seemingly race-blind rules also tended to disproportionately hurt black families. In most cities long residency requirements penalized recent migrants, who made up a substantial portion of most urban black communities. Even when black and white grants were equal, as they were in most northern cities, higher rents and food costs in overcrowded and exploited black neighborhoods meant the money could not go as far there.

Nevertheless, the overwhelmingly greater need of African Americans meant a greater proportion of the black than the white population did receive relief. In 1933 almost 20 percent of black urban dwellers relied on some form of aid, twice the proportion of whites. Most of these were families, not single individuals, testifying to the widespread desperation of the community. These numbers did not improve in subsequent years. By the start of 1935, almost one-third of all black families received financial help. Despite its racial imbalances, relief proved critical for the survival of hundreds of thousands of African Americans and their families.

Work programs that provided employment rather than financial aid had a similarly mixed record on race. Although work programs were more expensive, officials preferred them to direct relief, reasoning that paid employment was both more productive than handouts and better in sustaining self-respect. They had the added benefit of producing necessary public structures and services. Administered primarily through the PWA run by Harold Ickes and after 1935 by the WPA under Harry Hopkins, work programs changed the face of America. New post offices, airports, municipal and state buildings, park trails, farm windbreaks, low-cost housing, land reclamation, antiflooding projects, roads, and bridges built a new infrastructure for the nation in preparation for recovery.

Black communities benefited from such building projects, if not as much as white. Unemployed black workers needed jobs and black communities needed public facilities. Work programs helped meet both needs. More than $45 million of PWA funds were spent on building or improving black schools, hospitals, and the like, and another $5 million went to construct buildings at southern black colleges. Of the forty-nine PWA housing projects built between 1933 and 1937, fourteen were allocated to black tenants and another seventeen were integrated. Indeed Ickes compelled the PWA to allocate half of all southern public housing to African Americans. In some cities, such as Cleveland, African Americans actually received a disproportionate number of new housing units, although nowhere did the amount of new housing meet the need. The PWA also loaned money to cities and states; more than $20 million went to build 225 schools for black pupils, improve 118 more, and build or improve other facilities. While these projects met only a tiny portion of the need, they represented the most significant government commitment to black education to date.

For all their successes, however, in their hiring practices work programs proved even less equitable than direct relief, especially in the Depression's early years. Despite rules prohibiting discrimination, local projects administered by the PWA and other agencies routinely passed over African Americans for skilled jobs and offered them lower wages than whites for the same work in much of the South. Even where black and white workers received the same wages for their work, black workers were more often hired for shorter, temporary jobs. In fact Weaver and Hastie set the PWA's racial quotas precisely because so many local building projects discriminated against skilled black workers.

Other New Deal programs targeted rural and agricultural communities, where the majority of African Americans still lived. The Agricultural Adjustment Act (AAA), established in 1933, paid farmers subsidies so they could limit crop production. Lowering production, officials hoped, would both bolster farm prices and encourage conservation and soil improvement. The Civilian Conservation Corps (CCC) employed young people, primarily in the South and West, to protect and improve federal and state land and to counter soil erosion and other threats. The Tennessee Valley Authority (TVA) coordinated that region's water supply and turned it into a major power producer.

But many of these programs actually hurt black farmers, who bore the brunt of the production cutbacks and faced discrimination in the allocation of aid, jobs, and resources. In the early years of the AAA, landowners kept the government subsidies for themselves rather than distribute them to their tenants and sharecroppers. The NAACP spent more time in 1934 on this issue than any other. Finally, protests compelled the agency to make the payments directly to affected farmworkers.

The implementation of these programs offers a clear illustration of how institutional racism operated. Given widespread southern black disfranchisement, black farmers had no voice in the administration of the programs. Agency heads selected politically active and economically successful individuals for local leadership positions in order to give the programs maximum credibility. This made good political sense, but it meant that the landowners themselves or those who shared their interests ran the projects. Because crop allotment and other such decisions were locally determined, racism and existing power hierarchies played a strong role in the selection of what land to lie fallow or which family's production to cut. Not surprisingly, local officials generally threw black families out or cut their crops first, shifting thousands into more poorly paid farm wage labor or off the land entirely. The AAA also eased credit for farmers. This allowed landowners to invest in more mechanization tools, which in turn displaced still more farmworkers. The desperation of these dispossessed led to protests and the organization of the Sharecroppers' Union and the Southern Tenant Farmers' Union in 1934, but for the most part such protests were isolated and violently suppressed.

The CCC routinely hired whites first and generally brought electricity, telephones, park areas, or other services to white neighborhoods before black. Although the act creating the CCC prohibited discrimination by race, and more than twice as many black young men as white were unemployed, proportionately fewer black youths received CCC placement. In the CCC's first year, only 5 percent of all enrollees were black. Mississippi, with a majority black population, granted African Americans less than 2 percent of its CCC positions. Two Georgia counties whose black populations topped 60 percent selected no African Americans at all. Similar patterns emerged in rural Florida and Arkansas. When questioned, authorities explained that local whites received the slots because they were the neediest.

In deference to local custom, most CCC camps were segregated. Only New England and a few other locales provided integrated camps. When Wisconsin administrators requested permission to do the same, CCC director Robert Fechner denied it. In 1935 Fechner made the segregation requirement universal, explaining that segregation was not the same as discrimination and thus did not violate antidiscrimination rules. Segregation did lessen potential racial friction in the camps, but it created its own problems for black enrollees. Towns close to black camps protested that they posed a danger to residents and insisted that in any case those spaces should go to needy white youths. Nor did segregation offer black men opportunities for administrative positions. Even in all-black camps, those jobs went to whites.

The TVA proved among the worst in its record on race. Established in 1933 to coordinate the use of more than 42,000 square miles of land and water, TVA provided jobs, housing, recreational land, electricity, and greater navigation and flood control to one of the poorest areas in the country. Erosion and flooding had damaged much of the soil. The local average farm income, $639, was only approximately one-third of national farm income in 1930, and black tenant farmers on average earned only $140 annually, half that of what white tenants earned.

TVA became the largest employer in the area in its history, but African Americans benefited far less from it than whites. John Davis and Charles Houston of the NAACP reported in 1933 that not a single African American held a clerical position there or worked as a foreman. This was no surprise: TVA vocational and foreman training programs excluded black trainees. TVA officials did agree to hire African Americans equal to their proportion in the local population, 11 percent, and managed to hew fairly closely to that figure. But they did so primarily by hiring black workers only for menial and temporary jobs. The combined earnings of all TVA's unskilled black workers came to less than 1 percent of the TVA's total expenditure on wages. Equally troubling, despite official statements opposing discrimination, labor crews were racially segregated everywhere, in deference to the preferences of both TVA officials and local trade unions.

TVA proved no better at serving black residents' or black workers' needs. It built new residential communities for its white workers, but it did not allow any African Americans to live there except in temporary barracks. Elsewhere TVA communities were segregated by race, with black workers relegated, as usual, to the least desirable areas with the fewest and poorest services. Local white communities received power, parks, beaches, and other amenities more quickly than black. Certainly the TVA reflected racial practices rather than worsened them. But it did not live up to its own promise of providing work and opportunity based on equity and merit.

TVA offers another illustration of institutional racism in operation. The discrimination in access to new housing, project hiring, and promotions was not simply the result of choices made by individual whites, but rather was contained within the structure of TVA itself. The agency's system of hierarchies, unexamined assumption of white supremacy, deference to local norms, favoritism, and fear of conflict combined to ensure that no one would challenge the well-established racial order, allowing whites to benefit disproportionately from these programs. Embedded within the deepest structures of American society, institutional racism operated in much the same way everywhere, permitting discriminatory habits to go unchallenged and racist choices to be made unthinkingly even when they were not made deliberately.

In the spring of 1935 the Joint Committee on National Recovery and Ralph Bunche, head of Howard University's Division of Social Sciences, organized a conference on "The Position of the Negro in the Present Economic Crisis." Participants included representatives from black unions, liberal and progressive political organizations, and religious, sororal, and fraternal groups. The conference was unanimous in condemning virtually every New Deal program as not serving the interests of black people. Black workers, conference members asserted, were in some cases faring even more poorly than they had before. As they concluded, "The Negro worker has good reason to feel that his government has betrayed him under the New Deal."[1]

Much of the problem lay in the political nature of the New Deal itself. Because these programs were political creatures, they responded best to political pressure. Organized voices, such as labor or southern segregationist politicians, therefore proved more successful at getting what they wanted than did politically weaker communities like African Americans. It was this reality—that political pressure was an effective tool—that helped spur organizing efforts in so many black communities. The Joint Committee on National Recovery was itself part of this politicizing process. Thus the very failures of the New Deal led to its improvement as black pressure groups emerged to fight the political establishment on its own terms.

In many ways, 1935 proved a turning point for the New Deal. In that year the conservative Supreme Court declared several federal programs, including the NRA and FERA, unconstitutional. It ruled against the AAA a year later. A frustrated and angry Roosevelt regrouped, working with advisers and colleagues in and out of government to create new programs they hoped would pass constitutional muster. These proved not only more durable, but also more politically progressive and far more responsive to black needs.

Roosevelt's own pronouncements on race illustrated the change. He spoke out more often and more forcefully after 1935. He had certainly heard the urgings of his black and white advisers and was mindful of the very public criticism of both liberals and leftists regarding the failures of earlier New Deal agencies. But the leftward shift of the new programs was also facilitated by Roosevelt's political frustration with southern Democrats, who, despite his concessions to their views on race and on local control, continued to challenge the programs he had built. Furthermore, the continued opposition of business leaders to his policies and recalcitrance of the Supreme Court suggested that he could not reassure conservatives, and should not compromise his plans to try to do so.

Other political realities also moved the president from conciliation to more forceful action. The slowness of the economy to recover despite the early New Deal programs, the growing importance of the (primarily northern) black vote, the activism of the president's wife Eleanor Roosevelt, the appointment of liberal Supreme Court justices Felix Frankfurter and William O. Douglas and later Frank Murphy, the rise of the racist Nazi regime in Germany, and the rhetoric of the New Deal itself all contributed to improving the way the New Deal addressed the challenges of racism and the needs of black people.

The engagement of Eleanor Roosevelt in civil rights played a key role in improving the federal government's record on race. Using the public platform provided by her status as first lady, Mrs. Roosevelt took every opportunity to speak out on the issue. She called on her husband and Congress to improve New Deal programs with respect to race and to address discrimination, segregation, and lynching head on. With her encouragement Roosevelt appointed the first black federal judge, William Hastie, and first black assistant U.S. attorney general, William Houston (father of civil rights attorney Charles Houston). She lobbied government agencies to appropriate more money for black facilities like hospitals, schools, and housing projects and to enforce antidiscrimination provisions in government hiring. When black leaders found it difficult to convince white officials to meet with them, the first lady facilitated the meetings herself.

Most important in bringing about these changes, though, was the activism of African Americans at every level of public life. The number and clout of Roosevelt's advisers on civil rights, dubbed the "Black Cabinet" by the press, had increased dramatically in the early years of the New Deal. Ickes and Foreman remained engaged, but by 1935 African Americans in the administration provided the momentum. They included political veterans Robert Vann (now in the Justice Department), Eugene Kinckle Jones, William Pickens, Mary McLeod Bethune, Robert Weaver, and many young African American scholars including Rayford Logan, Ralph Bunche, William Trent Jr., and Frank Horne.

The group met weekly at Bethune's house to share information and ideas. Often they were joined by other black leaders including the NAACP's Walter White, John Davis of the Joint Committee on National Recovery, and labor leader A. Philip Randolph. Their broad reach within the administration, their large constituency, and the public nature of their engagement brought these men and women a great deal of political influence and began to change the nature of governmental response to black concerns. Sometimes they managed to insert antidiscrimination measures in legislation, integrate federal facilities or meetings, or expand the number of positions open to black job seekers. More often, they had smaller successes, like convincing an administrator not to institute a racist policy or keeping a white politician from making an overtly racist public comment. They encouraged newspapers, magazines, and radio to cover black concerns. Even when these black officials had little impact on program decisions per se, their intervention was crucial. They set an expectation that government officials would address the concerns of black people. They demonstrated that a mobilized black community could have political leverage. They made civil rights a public, if not a popular, news topic.

This activism at the top was supported by a similar organizing energy from below. Thousands of black community organizations, devoted to self-help during the early, desperate years of the Depression, shifted their focus to politics as the advantages of organizing became increasingly evident. While still providing food, clothing, and services to the poor, they also pressured New Deal agencies and local governments to respond to black needs. The relationship between community mobilization and national politics was nowhere clearer than in the career of Adam Clayton Powell Jr. In the course of little over a decade, Powell moved from activist minister of Harlem's Abyssinian Baptist Church to march organizer to city councilman to congressional representative. For Powell, and for the black community as a whole, aiding the poor shifted from a personal virtue to a political agenda in this era. Roosevelt based his New Deal on the premise that government had an obligation to aid all its citizens. Black community organizations considered it their duty to see to it that this obligation was fulfilled.

Meanwhile national civil rights organizations like the NAACP and the National Council of Negro Women pressed Congress and the president to ensure that qualified black applicants received appropriate employment, that African Americans on relief received the same benefits as whites, that antidiscrimination provisions were inserted in New Deal regulations, and that open racists did not receive federal appointments. Each helped move the New Deal toward greater inclusion.

Many of the resulting changes in New Deal programs, often called the Second New Deal, dramatically improved the lives of black people. The new Social Security and labor legislation of 1935 aided black workers, retirees, and the disabled. The new Works Progress Administration (WPA) hired and trained thousands of African Americans. Generally, these programs were more economically and politically radical than those that had come earlier. They supported unions more strongly, intervened more extensively in the economy, more vigorously protected the most vulnerable, and expanded opportunities for scholarly research and artistic expression. The Second New Deal cemented an uneasy Democratic coalition of southern whites, the working class, liberals, labor, and racial and ethnic minorities that would remain dominant for decades.

Still, in part because of the shakiness of that coalition, Roosevelt never pressed as forcefully as he might have for civil rights advances. Nor did he fully enforce regulations barring discrimination. It is not clear he could have, but more forceful use of his office as a "bully pulpit" certainly would have put the administration more explicitly on the side of racial justice. As a result, despite substantial improvements, black applicants to New Deal programs continued to fare worse than whites all over the United States, and especially in the South. Racial imbalances in relief did not improve substantially until 1939 when Congress amended the Emergency Relief Act to mandate equal treatment for all applicants regardless of race or religion. Even then, racist local administrators found ways around the rules. Still, the number of African Americans on relief, and the amounts they received, improved during Roosevelt's second term. Hundreds of thousands of needy black families survived economic devastation because of such government assistance.

One new form of relief came from the Social Security Act. Passed by Congress in 1935, it provided financial support for the elderly, the disabled, and the unemployed. A crucial bulwark of the welfare state, Social Security provided the difference between starvation and survival for millions of Americans of all races. Equally important was the implicit acknowledgment that government was responsible for the welfare of all its citizens. However, two elements of the act hurt black people substantially. As with other New Deal programs, states received the funds to disburse on the assumption that local officials understood local needs best. This policy, of course, eased the way for racist administrators to shortchange black applicants or deny their requests. Thousands of such complaints reached the ears of federal officials. Worse,

Congress acquiesced to demands that domestic and agricultural workers be excluded from receiving Social Security benefits—two employment fields in which African Americans remained overrepresented. These two exclusions alone denied coverage to 65 percent of African Americans. Black women suffered most of all. Social Security covered only 30 percent of white working women but an even tinier fraction of black women, 16 percent.

The Second New Deal's major new work relief program greatly expanded the government's reach into black communities. To the extent possible, the WPA, like the PWA, employed people at the trades at which they actually worked, although the pay scales were deliberately set lower than those in private industry. Needy families received shoes made by government-funded cobblers, audiences watched shows performed by government-funded actors. The social and physical benefits were enormous to both the newly reemployed and those who enjoyed what they produced.

More than 5,000 black instructors worked in the WPA Education Program, teaching close to a quarter of a million black children and adults. Black repertory groups organized under the auspices of the Federal Theatre Project bringing classic and original works to black audiences around the country who had little other access to drama. Often these shows had sharp political edges, challenging racism or political repression, or celebrating the successes of historical black heroes. In Harlem audiences enjoyed an all-black *Macbeth*; across the country these theater groups brought the stories of Harriet Tubman and Nat Turner to life. The Theatre Project also offered "living newspapers" that explored current events, including politically charged issues like lynching. The Federal Art Project not only ornamented public spaces with murals and sculptures by black as well as white artists, but also set up schools where artists and musicians taught their skills to children and the unemployed. Painters Jacob Lawrence and Gwendolyn Knight studied there. The Federal Music Project performed works by new composers, both black and white, and recorded local musicians playing gospel, jazz, and blues. The Federal Writers Project (FWP) and its Historical Records Survey hired struggling authors and researchers to gather folklore of different ethnic and racial groups (author Zora Neale Hurston collected southern black folktales and music, for example); interview former slaves; and provide information for a large number of bibliographies and regional guides. Ralph Ellison and Richard Wright first published with the FWP. Other FWP participants included poet Margaret Walker and John Johnson who later published *Ebony* and *Jet* magazines.

The most thorough study of the Depression-era black community ever done also relied on these funds. In 1937 the Carnegie Foundation invited the

Swedish sociologist Gunnar Myrdal to study the conditions of African Americans. With substantial WPA support, hundreds of scholars and researchers collected and evaluated data on black life and history, from health and employment to cultural production and family structure. Nearly half of the scholars were African American, including Ira DeAugustine Reid, Allison Davis, St. Clair Drake, Horace Cayton, Charles Johnson, E. Franklin Frazier, Abram Harris, Benjamin Quarles, Ralph Bunche, Carter Woodson, Rayford Logan, and Robert Weaver, all leading academics in their fields. The product of this research included hundreds of reports and studies, many later synthesized in a number of books including Richard Sterner's *The Negro's Share* (1943) on black income, housing, and consumption; Drake and Cayton's *Black Metropolis* about Chicago (1945); and Myrdal's magisterial *American Dilemma* (1944), filled with data on the black community over time.

Every WPA contract required that the number of African Americans hired be proportionately equal to their number in the most recent occupational census. The Housing Authority and several others implemented similar requirements. More actively enforced during the Second New Deal, these measures increased the number of African Americans in skilled positions, as well as their pay, and brought them into several unions. By the end of 1936 close to 20 percent of WPA workers were black, many of them in job categories appropriate to their skill level. In cities like Cleveland, African Americans made up almost a third of the total WPA labor force. In fact, by the end of the decade, as whites increasingly found employment, the proportion of relief recipients who were African American climbed. In 1940 the unemployment rate stood at 20 percent for African American men and 11 percent for white. It made sense, then, that 15 percent of black male workers in the North, and fewer than 5 percent of white, held WPA-type "emergency employment." The PWA also showed dramatic improvement. By 1936 African Americans made up close to 16 percent of the agency's skilled labor force and 21 percent of the semiskilled. By the end of the decade almost a third of all wages paid by the PWA went to black workers.

Ironically, in cities like New York and Chicago quotas actually limited black opportunities because the number of available black workers exceeded the number of positions set aside for them. These men and women found themselves in unskilled positions, if they found any relief work at all. In Cleveland, for example, while 17 percent of black respondents holding WPA jobs reported that they had formerly done skilled work, less than 1 percent were employed in such positions in the WPA. For the 20 percent of black female WPA workers there who had previously done skilled work, less than half a percent held skilled jobs in WPA projects.

The Works Progress Administration often provided job training for African Americans in fields that fit white officials' idea of what jobs were appropriate or available for black workers. Here, young men attending a WPA training class in Arizona in 1936 serve the white WPA and U.S. Employment Service officials posing as diners. Courtesy of the Franklin D. Roosevelt Library Digital Archives.

Elsewhere, particularly in the South, local white leaders continued to hire black workers only for menial labor positions regardless of their actual skill level or the availability of skilled positions. Others simply refused to hire any black people at all so long as there were white people in need of work. Access to WPA jobs was even more limited for rural black southerners. The WPA's internal hiring practices reflected the same patterns. While African Americans obtained administrative positions in many northern cities, of the more than 10,000 WPA supervisory officials in the South, only 11 were black.

The consequences of these agencies' policies often reinforced segregation. Although Ickes had seen to it that black people occupied close to a third of all PWA housing, few of those projects were built in integrated neighborhoods. Half of those designated for African Americans were built in existing black slum areas. The U.S. Housing Authority followed a similar pattern. Although a significant number of units did go to black tenants, most remained in segregated buildings in segregated neighborhoods. Institutional racism was again at work. The decision to place black housing in existing black areas reflected a desire to minimize racial strife and respect the wishes of the current residents of white neighborhoods. But such choices, reasonable on their face, perpetuated the inequalities established long before. Even as white agency leaders prided themselves on helping needy black families, they simultaneously reinforced the segregation and discrimination that limited the opportunities of those same families.

This was not how most African Americans viewed the WPA, however. Despite discrimination, public work programs provided employment to more than a million African American workers and their families. Perhaps pay rates were lower than what many private sector jobs offered, but few black people could get those jobs in any case. Everywhere, WPA wages were higher than the average earnings of privately employed black workers. Thousands obtained skills and experience through the WPA they could get nowhere else, and all were saved from complete financial ruin. Both children and adults benefited from the goods and services provided by WPA workers, from decent housing at reasonable rents to health care. Thousands of older black adults learned to read. The public buildings built by the WPA, though often segregated, provided desperately needed infrastructure in black communities around the country from schools to playgrounds, from hospitals to community centers. Such investments impressed black communities who had not received any governmental attention whatever before this point.

The Second New Deal also strengthened the position of labor. That the Congress of Industrial Organizations was founded in 1935, the year Congress passed the Wagner National Labor Relations Act, was no coincidence. By reaffirming the right of collective bargaining, prohibiting the formation of company unions, and establishing a National Labor Relations Board for oversight and mediation between unions and employers, the act opened up new possibilities for organizing. It particularly aided unskilled industrial workers like those in steel, mining, automotive, and longshore trades. Leftist-led unions and virtually all those seeking to organize the unskilled included explicit antidiscrimination clauses in their bylaws, and some locals elected black officers. Individual locals often disregarded national mandates in favor of local traditions, but the struggle for racial equality on the shop floor had been engaged.

The plight of sharecroppers and farm tenants compelled new federal programs for rural areas as well, especially after the publicity generated by the Southern Tenant Farmers' Union. The Rural Electrification Act (1935) brought running water and electricity to thousands who lacked it. Roosevelt also created the Resettlement Administration in 1935, succeeded by the

Farm Security Administration (FSA) in 1937. The FSA primarily provided loans to farmworkers. Largely thanks to the efforts of its director, Will Alexander, the FSA helped hundreds of African American farmers buy land of their own and thousands more to rehabilitate their holdings. FSA funds also allowed black farmers to decrease their reliance on exploitative planters for seed and credit, which dramatically cut their debt. According to the Department of Agriculture, as a result of such programs the average net worth of black farm families rose from $451 in 1936 to $752 in 1938. Alexander also fought hard to increase the number of black supervisors and the number and amount of loans given to black families.

Still, the net impact on black farming communities was negative. Although the program increased the number of white farm owners, it did not have the same result for African Americans. Because the FSA sought to help small farmers rather than large landowners, it did not enjoy the same level of support by southern political leaders and was never adequately funded. As a result, the loans were too small for those so deeply in debt, and administrators granted fewer of them to African American farmers. Of all black farmers on relief or earning less than $500 a year, 11 percent received FSA loans, compared with 22 percent of similarly poor white farmers. The size of those grants also differed. Taking 1939 as an example, whites received an average loan of $685, while African Americans received $606. Once again, good intentions from the top improved the lives of many black families but could not level the playing field. The structural impediments, compounded by the racism of local administrators, proved insurmountable.

Substantial federal pressure did finally raise the number of black enrollees in the CCC during the Second New Deal. The proportion of CCC workers who were black rose from 6 percent in 1935 to almost 10 percent a year later. Still, it took longer for African Americans to receive skilled or administrative placements, and the camps remained segregated. In 1936, after protests over the virtual impossibility for African Americans to obtain high-level positions in CCC camps, FDR called for the CCC to appoint black supervisors whenever possible. The statement was so vague, however, that little in fact changed. The number of black supervisors in black camps did not increase substantially until 1938, when the number of black enrollees also rose again, to reach 11 percent of the total CCC workforce. In July 1942 the CCC closed its doors. In its nine years, 2.5 million men passed through CCC camps, not quite 200,000 of them African American.

Black youths fared better with the National Youth Administration (NYA), set up in 1935 as part of the WPA. The NYA provided money that allowed young people in needy families to stay in school. Headed by sympathetic

Aubrey Williams, and ably assisted by Mary McLeod Bethune as administrator of Negro Affairs, more than 600,000 African American youths and their families received help they desperately needed. In 1920 only 53 percent of African Americans ages five to twenty were enrolled in school. The combination of programs like the NYA and the lack of jobs increased that figure to 64 percent by 1940. Considering only higher education (ages fifteen to twenty), the number of African Americans enrolled jumped 5 percent from 1930 to 1940. Virtually every black college received some NYA aid. The NYA also insisted on equal pay in its work programs and admitted African Americans to all its skilled training programs. More than 60,000 black young people received such training. All told, the NYA served 300,000 black students, 11 percent of the total number receiving aid.

Bethune also used the agency to coordinate broader efforts on behalf of African Americans. For example, she organized two widely attended confer-

The Negro Youth Administration generally provided more equitable training for black and white young people. In this 1936 photo, young black women who have received clerical training are paid by the NYA to work at an Illinois branch of the "Colored" YWCA. Chicago, IL, 1936, Courtesy of the Franklin D. Roosevelt Library Digital Archives.

ences on "Problems of the Negro and Negro Youth" in 1937 and 1939. Each conference brought more than a hundred black and white activists and government officials together to evaluate the progress of black Americans and set agendas for the future. Their recommendations were presented to the president and guided participants in future policy making and agenda setting. Such forums for study, brainstorming, and planning sustained and expanded activism on behalf of racial equality.

The same forces that made New Deal programs more racially egalitarian also affected internal federal employment policies. The civil service underwent a sea change in its hiring practices. Beyond nondiscrimination guidelines, it dropped its requirement to submit a photo with a job application. As a result, the fewer than 50,000 black civil servants employed before Roosevelt's presidency grew to almost 200,000 by 1941, or 10 percent of the entire federal workforce. Even more impressive, many of these jobs were in areas still generally off limits to African Americans in private industry, including architecture, engineering, administration, law, stenography, economics, statistics, and chemistry.

Although the overwhelming majority of black federal employees still held menial and unskilled positions, most in the community celebrated these developments. The difficulty in obtaining professional or skilled work was nothing new, but the relative openness of the federal government, and the stability such jobs offered, were. Local government jobs also became available in several cities with large black populations, as municipal bureaucracies expanded. Chicago, New York, and other large northern cities proved increasingly willing to hire black workers, both because their leaders were more progressive and because their black communities had become better organized and more effective in exerting political pressure.

There can be no question that New Deal programs transformed African Americans' lives. Government aid saved millions from unemployment, starvation, and eviction. These programs provided jobs and training, income, housing, and education. They kept families together and young people in school. Not only did black individuals and their families benefit from these programs, so did African American communities as a whole. New Deal money funded day care centers, art programs, and housing projects and allowed researchers to evaluate black community needs, record oral histories of former slaves, and document black folklife.

The New Deal's psychological contributions to the African American community were as important as the physical improvements it brought. For the first time since Reconstruction, the government paid attention to black people. And for the first time in the nation's history, the federal government acknowledged explicitly that it owed a basic living standard to all its citizens.

As Roy Wilkins concluded in the pages of the NAACP's *Crisis* magazine, the "most important contribution of the Roosevelt administration to the age-old color line problem in America has been its doctrine that Negroes are a part of the country and must be considered in any program for the country as a whole. . . . For the first time in their lives, government has taken on meaning and substance for the Negro masses."[2]

On the other hand, the New Deal provided less of everything to black people than to white: less funding, fewer services, worse jobs, and a lower proportion of the needy served. By any objective measure African Americans were poorer, less well educated, more disadvantaged, and more desperate. They received not only less than they needed, but proportionately less than whites. The New Deal did not—perhaps could not—overcome the racism, both personal and structural, that kept black people locked into second-class citizenship.

In short, the record of work and direct relief agencies was distinctly mixed for black people. Millions of African Americans received help who had never received it before, but they benefited less than did their white neighbors, and racism remained endemic in every program. These realities energized black political activism, but that activism actually brought only limited changes during the Depression decade. Gatherings of black leaders and organizations from NAACP conferences to the more informal meetings in Mary McLeod Bethune's home, from the National Negro Congress to the 1942 annual meeting of the National Urban League, reached the same conclusions over and over again. The New Deal had made significant inroads into black poverty and lessened racial discrimination, but in the end it had not been enough. These findings summarize well the ambivalent legacy of President Roosevelt's New Deal.

Notes

1. Quoted from Ronald Takaki, *Double Victory: A Multicultural History of America in World War II* (Boston: Back Bay Press, 2000), 39.

2. Roy Wilkins, "The Roosevelt Record," *The Crisis* 47, no. 11 (November 1940): 343.

CHAPTER FOUR

~

"Let Us Build": Political Organizing in the Depression Era

Out of the New Deal came a greater political engagement and mobilization in black communities across the country. Locally and nationally, black activists, whether Democrat or Republican, liberal, left, or nationalist, expanded their range of tactics and approaches. Self-help groups became increasingly political as they came to understand the new potential to improve conditions through public and electoral pressure. Organizations already political in orientation seized the new possibilities of the moment to expand and redefine their missions and their strategies. Tactics varied by location and by issue: most mobilized pragmatically to attain realistic goals. That meant something different in small towns than in large cities, in the South than in the North or West. But everywhere, black communities responded to both the challenges hardship posed and the possibilities politics offered.

The same African American organizations and political leaders galvanized by the promises of the New Deal protested its inequities. Communities mobilized to improve local conditions and support national campaigns. Liberal and progressive white and interracial organizations often lent their expertise, financial support, and public visibility to the cause, including the National Council of Jewish Women, Congress of Industrial Organizations, National Farmers' Union, National Women's Trade Union League, International Ladies Garment Workers' Union, Workmen's Circle, Catholic Worker Movement, American Jewish Congress, American Civil Liberties Union, and dozens of others. Groups further left like the National Lawyers' Guild,

American Labor Party, and the Socialist and Communist Parties embraced these efforts as well.

Constrained by racism and the threat of violence—particularly although not exclusively in the South—such engagement was often faltering and rarely threatened the basic structures underlying discrimination or segregation. Nevertheless, political organizing on every scale provided a training ground for activists and a laboratory for tactics that would prove invaluable in the future. It also provided the momentum for a growing black electoral engagement that, coupled with continued migration into urban areas, meant northern black communities had become political forces to be reckoned with. It was in the Great Depression that national black voting patterns turned solidly Democratic, as African Americans "turn[ed] Lincoln's picture to the wall," in the words of Robert Vann, publisher of the *Pittsburgh Courier*.[1] In many ways black political action redefined itself during the Depression decade.

This political mobilization also produced a clearer roadmap for future action and more explicit articulations of a black civil rights agenda. The 1937 and 1939 conferences Mary McLeod Bethune organized produced a list of goals that presaged the civil rights movement of the 1950s and 1960s, including federal anti-lynching legislation, full and equal access to the ballot, and an end to segregation and to economic and residential discrimination. The NAACP reorganized its litigation department and pioneered new approaches. The political momentum spurred the creation of the National Negro Congress in 1936 to coordinate civil rights activities. Although it could not sustain itself in the long term, it too offered a clear list of goals future activists would pursue.

The explosive growth of black political activism was plain to see in the 1930s, in the expansion of traditional forms of communication and action, and in the formation of new organizations and new agendas. Traditional forms of communication such as black newspapers and congregational sermons combined with newer vehicles. In much of the rural South owning or reading any explicitly political material could prove dangerous. Elsewhere, however, local political groups produced an increasing number of pamphlets and broadsides to disseminate information or propaganda, and street corner orators preached publicly about the problems facing black people. Street demonstrations, protest pickets, coalition building, and lobbying campaigns helped turn speech into public action.

Black newspapers—at least 227 were publishing regularly in 1938—continued to serve both a local and a national audience hungry for information, from the St. Louis Argus to the Norfolk Journal and Guide. Several new black papers began publishing in this decade as well, including the *Birmingham World* in 1931 and the *Los Angeles Sentinel* in 1933. Spurred by a reenergized local NAACP chapter, the *Evansville* (Indiana) *Argus* started publishing in 1938. Despite the economic difficulties, circulation figures actually rose through the decade. In 1936, for example, the *Chicago Defender* reported an impressive 73,000 subscribers. Four years later that number had risen to 82,000. The *Baltimore Afro-American* had 54,000 subscribers in Baltimore, and 95,500 in total. Widely shared, these and other black papers reached hundreds of thousands. Political developments, economic conditions, the limits and achievements of New Deal programs, advances in the workplace or in the courts, instances of racial oppression or racial advancement, the struggles of minority groups abroad under the yoke of Nazis or colonial powers—all were chronicled in these papers, as were debates over the relative merits of various strategies and approaches. Newspaper editorials and regular columns of political commentary ensured that the black press both reflected black political action and shaped it.

These conversations continued in the pages of black journals like the NAACP's *The Crisis* and the Urban League's *Opportunity* as well as in the publications and newsletters of smaller political organizations, who likewise offered both information and closely argued analysis to their audience. Increasingly, activists also took their messages to the streets, whether speaking from a soapbox on an urban corner or addressing mass demonstrations in front of government buildings. There were as many stories to tell as ways to tell them. Activist organizations, both liberal and radical, experimented with new forms and levels of activism as the decade unfolded. Coverage in the press and through public speeches served not only to educate the community, but also to increase the visibility of, and support for, the group doing the organizing. Both public engagement and organizational strength in turn increased the likelihood of success. Publicity mattered.

Individual white public figures helped advance and shape civil rights activism as well, perhaps none as much as the wife of the president. Eleanor Roosevelt's engagement went beyond advancing black interests in New Deal programs, crucial though that was. She also helped publicize the broader cause. Her close friendships with Walter White, executive secretary of the NAACP since 1931, and Mary McLeod Bethune brought her into sustained contact with the civil rights struggle and its many leaders. She defied local authorities to integrate segregated political meetings, participated in conferences on black education and welfare, and wrote and spoke across the country on economic and political issues important to African Americans from lynching to job discrimination. All this helped build and sustain black loyalty to the Democratic Party. More important, it advanced black equality.

Eleanor Roosevelt's symbolic gestures, as much as her political advocacy, made their own contribution to civil rights. Her public exhortations for racial justice and equal opportunity, her public embrace of African American friends and colleagues, and her presence at integrated social events—actions that horrified white supremacists—all pressed hard against the polite conventions of the day and made her an important role model for other progressive political leaders. In one of her most visible actions, she publicly resigned her membership in the prestigious Daughters of the American Revolution in 1939. That organization had refused to allow black contralto Marian Anderson, celebrated across Europe for her magnificent voice, to sing in its Constitution Hall. Walter White proposed that the federal government sponsor a public concert for her instead, and Eleanor became one of its most active organizers. She made sure that important government figures were present, from Supreme Court justices and Cabinet members to foreign diplomats and members of Congress, when Anderson sang to more than 75,000 people on the steps of the Lincoln Memorial on Easter Sunday, 1939.

The heightened engagement in political activism during the Depression was evident across the nation. Local coalitions among black and multiracial groups organized around issues of employment and residential discrimination, anti-black violence, and southern poll tax laws. In Seattle, for example, black community groups from Communists to Republicans, middle class and poor, united to protest a 1938 case of police brutality that resulted in the death of a black hotel waiter. Unlike most cases of white violence against blacks, the officers were convicted and sentenced to prison, although the governor later pardoned them. The Seattle branch of the NAACP blocked bills prohibiting intermarriage and brought cases of employment discrimination to court. Across the North and West, local campaigns won more and better jobs for black workers, some civil rights protections, greater municipal responsiveness to the needs of the black poor, and brought a number of important black electoral and victories. Northern activists expanded on their earlier efforts to increase the pace of change. More unexpectedly, significant organizing took place in the South, even though these attempts generally either failed or brought only limited success. The tools of advocacy, the expression of black discontent, and the increased willingness to mobilize were crucial steps in the building of a national movement for civil rights.

Although northern black writers like Langston Hughes criticized the apathy of their southern compatriots, there was a great deal of black community activism across the South. Generally such activities were quieter and less public than in the North, given the widespread white resistance to black advancement and the ever-present threat of violence, but they demonstrated to local whites that southern as well as northern black people had real aspirations to full citizenship and were willing to mobilize to achieve it.

Southern black communities organized for many reasons, such as equal pay, improved school conditions, or funding for community improvement projects. Most failed, but sometimes even setbacks prompted community response. Although the courts rejected a 1939 NAACP case challenging unequal pay for teachers in Norfolk, Virginia, the resulting firing of the black teacher named in the suit provoked public protest demonstrations from a community usually far less confrontational. Carrying signs equating the school board with Hitler and Mussolini and decrying violations of constitutional rights, school children marched while their angry parents organized petition drives demanding the teacher's reinstatement. Although their efforts failed, the case ultimately prevailed and the city and its black teachers agreed on a settlement. That settlement, much to the NAACP's disgust, was a compromise: the black teachers, accustomed to deference and conciliation, decided to take what they could for fear they would otherwise get nothing. Nevertheless, community activism suggested a vast and largely untapped potential for mass action that would prove the backbone of the coming civil rights movement. Meanwhile the NAACP continued its efforts. Taking up other cases of teacher pay inequity, the association soon won several victories in federal district courts.

Few Depression-era southern campaigns tapped that mass potential. They focused on specific issues and used tactics that were far more restrained. African Americans in Atlanta and several other southern cities, often led by their tiny middle class, pressed to increase funding for black schools, even if they could not improve teacher pay. School boards usually responded with more funds for buses to black schools or the building of a new gym or cafeteria. Historian Joe Trotter chronicled a five-year struggle on the part of Norfolk's black political leaders to convince the city to build a small—and segregated—beach. Interracial coalitions like the Commission on Interracial Cooperation proved just as conciliatory to southern racial norms. Its program to improve conditions for black Americans included building black library branches in several cities and holding annual interracial meetings in churches on "Race Relations Sunday," an event created in 1922 by the Federal Council of Churches to remind parishioners of the unity of mankind.

These limited successes raised difficult questions. Activists generally achieved them only by working with whites still committed to segregation. Thus, the Norfolk beaches remained segregated, allocations for education remained lopsided, and the schools remained separated by race. More often than not, the white leaders who enabled these improvements also fought against any union-organizing efforts, so important for black economic advancement. Were these necessary compromises for advancement, or did the acquiescence to white supremacy undermine whatever improvements had been won? As a final irony, many working-class whites who supported union struggles were often implacably opposed to even the segregated improvements supported by those white elites. The contradictions inherent in black political action in the South defied resolution, and African Americans divided over how best to proceed. Was cooperation with segregationist white elites a concrete improvement for black lives or a fatal collusion with the forces that oppressed them? Was organizing with whites who otherwise despised them an advance, or would any victory they won end up in a new system that proved equally exclusionary?

For many, the ever-present threat of white violence meant they could hope for no more than these small steps. So many campaigns met with intimidation and violence. When Minister B. J. Glover, educated in the North, tried to register to vote in his home county of Abbeville, South Carolina, in 1936, he was refused. His preaching about this experience and his broader activism on behalf of black interests came to the attention of the local Klan. In 1939 five Klansmen attacked him, beating and torturing him for hours before leaving him for dead. He survived and recuperated at home while armed neighbors took turns protecting his family from further attack. Black community action prevented further violence, but the attackers, known to the minister, were never arrested. In such a context, moderation and conciliation seemed to make sense. But in these cases, working within the existing political framework doomed the possibility of substantive change.

If black people could vote, they might be able to overcome some of these issues. Many local campaigns across the South therefore mobilized to expand black access to the ballot, even in the face of legal obstacles and the persistent threat of white violence. Two Atlanta coalitions took on the challenge in the early years of the Depression. They managed to place two black men on the ballot for citywide office in 1934, although neither won. African Americans in Alabama, South Carolina, and Texas challenged their exclusion from primary elections in 1934; none of these challenges succeeded.

In Birmingham in 1938 the Communist Party launched a Right to Vote Club. It prepared African Americans to register to vote teaching them how to fill out the required forms and how to prove that they met state eligibility requirements. Despite widespread fear, many tried to register but virtually all were rejected. The club and the NAACP filed discrimination complaints on behalf of those applicants who were willing to have their names made public. After arduous struggle the number of black registered voters grew from 700 to close to 3,000, but few could afford the annual poll taxes, and by 1940 the campaign admitted failure and disbanded. In Greenville, South Carolina, black civic organizations, with their mostly middle-class membership, launched their own voter registration drive in 1939. The Klan threatened violence, several activists were arrested, and few succeeded in registering. These struggles were important symbolically but not substantively. For example, the number of black Atlantans on the voting rolls did double between 1936 and 1939—but only from 1,000 to 2,000. As late as 1940, only 5 percent of black adults in the entire South were registered to vote.

In the few southern cities where African Americans could vote, their enforced residential clustering meant they could be a potent voting bloc. Such reasoning compelled even groups opposed to integration to press for greater black engagement in politics. In Norfolk, for example, where local elections were often hotly contested, even the nationalist and emigration-minded UNIA urged black residents to pay the poll tax so they could register to vote. In a few cities like San Antonio, Chattanooga, and Memphis, white political machines permitted or even encouraged black voting, so long as those votes were delivered for the "correct" candidate. In such situations black voters still had no meaningful voice.

The North, however, was another story. Given divisions among white voters, African Americans sometimes helped determine election results. Although African Americans constituted less than 4 percent of the total northern population, the high rate of segregation and black urbanization meant they formed potent voting blocs in numerous cities. Adam Clayton Powell Jr. became the first African American to serve on New York's City Council in 1942, and joined Congress as Harlem's representative in 1944. Black state legislators were also elected in California, Kansas, New Jersey, Pennsylvania, Illinois, West Virginia, Indiana, and Kentucky.

By and large, black voters in the North pulled the lever for Democrats. There, the Democratic Party proved far more engaged than Republicans in fighting the economic and racial problems black people faced. Indeed for local elections, some African Americans had already begun voting Democratic during the migration years, as that party's political machines aided black as well as white newcomers in order to win their votes. In New York and Chicago, the first significant black appointments well predated the New Deal. Roosevelt consolidated those gains and made them national. The New Deal, the active support the black community received from the president's wife, Eleanor, and the appointment of African Americans to high level government posts convinced the vast majority of black voters to abandon the Republican Party, Abraham Lincoln's political home, for the Democratic Party, as Robert Vann had urged them to do in 1932.

In that 1932 election, black newspapers were divided. The *Baltimore Afro-American, Norfolk Journal and Guide, Pittsburgh Courier*, and *Kansas City Call* endorsed Roosevelt; New York's *Amsterdam News*, the *Philadelphia Tribune*, and the *Cleveland Gazette* supported Hoover. While the black community proved equally divided in 1932, black approval of Democratic policies was reflected in the quickly shifting voting patterns. By 1934 the shift from Republican to Democrat was underway. Encouraged by Roosevelt's programs, and spurred on by black leaders eager to persuade these new progressive Democrats that support of civil rights would bring votes, African Americans in numerous cities rewarded candidates who saw to it that local black constituents also enjoyed the benefits of New Deal programs.

In Philadelphia black leaders collaborated with local Democrats to win electoral victories. In Missouri, Kansas City and St. Louis mayors appointed a larger number of African Americans to political positions than ever before. New York and Chicago mayors appointed black judges, aldermen, committeemen, and district leaders. In Chicago, the Democratic machine even ran a black candidate against the popular black Republican congressman Oscar DePriest. When Arthur Mitchell won that election in 1934, he became the first black Democrat ever to serve in Congress. At that point half of all African American voters chose Democrats. By 1936 Roosevelt and the Democrats were winning more than 70 percent of the black vote. Ironically, Robert Vann himself withdrew his support of the Democrats in 1940. As Republicans caught on to the power of black votes, and as white southern Democrats continued to block progressive legislation, Vann backed Republican Wendell Wilkie for president. By then, however, black voters had turned firmly Democratic, and few African Americans heeded Vann's advice. Indeed the loyalty of African Americans to the Democratic Party lasted beyond the end of the twentieth century.

Even in the South, progressive Democrats wooed African Americans during the Depression. A new interracial group, the Southern Conference for Human Welfare (SCHW), organized in 1938, hoping to harness the new political energy in black communities for the Democratic Party. Black and white southern liberals and leftists, many of them New Deal administrators and CIO leaders, gathered in Birmingham to discuss the *Report on the Economic Conditions of the South*, prepared by the New Deal's National Emergency Council. Given the multitude of challenges the report identified, they agreed on the need for a new, activist, interracial organization to expand political and economic opportunities for African Americans in that region. Southern Democratic Party leaders, mired in white supremacist ideologies, had been moving away from Roosevelt's New Deal as it had increasingly embraced minority concerns. SCHW organizers hoped that by strengthening and democratizing southern economic and political life, and including African Americans in it, they might solidify a new progressive base for the southern Democratic Party. Holding interracial meetings from the start—at its first Birmingham meeting Eleanor Roosevelt challenged the city's segregated seating rules by placing her chair directly in the aisle between the two sections—SCHW concentrated on fighting the poll tax and other voting restrictions; fostering union organizing and collective bargaining; improving health and social services for black communities; building support for anti-lynching legislation; and challenging economic discrimination against African Americans, Mexicans, Jews, and other marginalized groups. SCHW often relied on coalitions to expand its reach and build new political connections. Its local and national campaigns against the poll tax, for example, not only enlisted local support, but also brought in the NAACP, National Council of Negro Women, National Council of Jewish Women, and other national organizations. Nevertheless, their efforts came to nothing.

Although the Communist Party in this period called for a Popular Front strategy of working with liberal groups, including the Democratic Party, when their interests coincided, it nonetheless largely rejected both political parties. Communists argued that black civil rights could only be achieved by combining that struggle with one for workers' rights, and only an integrated, united working class could bring about fundamental change. Although the Communist International had advocated a separate black-controlled area in the South and had even cooperated with Garvey in the 1920s, in practice, Communists fought for full integration of African Americans into the workplace and national civic life.

Much of the Communist Party's activity took place in Unemployment Councils (UC), specifically organized by the party to mobilize desperate job seekers and their families. In Baltimore, New York, St. Louis, Cleveland, Detroit, Birmingham, Pittsburgh, Washington, D.C., New Orleans, Los Angeles, Chicago, and hundreds of smaller cities, UCs held rallies demanding better municipal services, more generous relief allocations and reduced rents. They launched rent strikes against landlords who refused to improve their rundown properties and led protests on behalf of victims of racism. In northern cities, where segregation was not mandated by law, Communists and other progressive organizations also fought to require that all new housing projects accept both black and white tenants in all buildings.

Perhaps most visible to local communities, councils around the country came to the aid of those evicted for nonpayment of rent. Especially during the early Depression years, such events occurred regularly. During some months large cities like Chicago and New York saw up to twenty evictions a day. Upon learning that a dispossessed family's possessions had been deposited outside the building, UC members would gather and return the belongings to the apartment. Neighbors and friends often joined them, as well as other poor families worried about their own futures. Given the economic vulnerability of the black community, hundreds came out to support these dramatic public efforts. Sometimes they became impromptu demonstrations.

Many UCs made a difference in the lives of the needy. Hosea Hudson described helping those turned down for relief in Birmingham by organizing a small group to return to the office and politely but firmly press matters further. Often, simply the display of community support persuaded officials to change their position. In New York a UC, along with other Communist groups, improved the treatment of African American applicants to the Home Relief Bureau, both in levels of courtesy and in rates of support.

More often, however, these actions, like those of interracial union organizing, were met with violence. Police attacked black protesters at Winston-Salem and Washington, D.C., demonstrations in 1930. An Unemployment Council in Greenville, South Carolina, comprised of both races led protests, rallies, and demonstrations for jobs, relief, and food beginning in February 1931, attended by dissatisfied citizens of both races. By April, protesters faced Klan attacks and similar violence. By September, the protests had halted altogether. In Norfolk, almost 1,000 black families launched a rent strike in 1932 but arrests, fines, violence, and the lack of support by white tenants led to the strike's collapse.

Similar patterns of protest and violence occurred across the nation. Those returning the possessions of evicted families to their homes in Chicago, Detroit, New York, Philadelphia, Seattle, and elsewhere routinely clashed with police. Even in the North, black protesters bore the brunt of the violence. When New York City police attacked protesters in two Communist-led interracial demonstrations, the *New York Times* observed that officers had predominantly targeted black people. Likewise, state troopers attacked black protesters in Albany, New York.

In Chicago, the summer of 1931 brought lethal violence. Local UCs returned dozens of evicted families to their homes in July. After protests from landlords, police surrounded activists restoring furniture to an apartment on August 3. Both protesters and police accused the other of attacking first; by the end of the melee three black men had been killed and twenty-one arrested. The Communist Party held nightly demonstrations until the funerals that attracted thousands. The mayor, who blamed Communists for the violence, nonetheless declared a temporary halt in evictions.

As the Chicago events suggest, even protests that provoked violence could succeed. In St. Louis, the familiar pattern of demonstration met by repression led to a restoration of relief in 1932. Mayors around the country capitulated to protest demands, increasing relief allocations, raising municipal pay rates, or temporarily halting evictions. In the end, these acts did not change the level of desperation much. But they did demonstrate the potential of organized community action.

All this activity won the Communist Party adherents in the black community, including prominent scholars and activists like writers Richard Wright and Langston Hughes (although both later left), and lawyer, journalist, and longtime organizer Benjamin Davis. Actor and singer Paul Robeson, perhaps the most famous of those sympathetic to the Communist Party, used his considerable musical and dramatic talents to advocate for the rights of all those oppressed, although such outspokenness cost him dearly in his professional life. He spoke publicly and gave concerts and performances on behalf of African Americans, exploited workers, Jews in areas under Nazi control, Spanish Loyalists who opposed the dictator Francisco Franco, and other communities under siege. In response, the FBI kept him under surveillance for three decades, the State Department revoked his passport, film distributors refused to handle his movies, halls canceled his performances, and an anti-Communist mob attacked him and his audience at an outdoor concert.

Especially during the Popular Front years, Communists sought collaboration with non-Communist activist organizations. As the CP reached out to more moderate and liberal civil rights groups, they in turn often proved willing to collaborate as they recognized the effectiveness of Communist tactics and strategies. Following the successful work of the party with New York's Home Relief Bureau, for example, the NAACP, several churches, and the *Amsterdam News* joined the effort to challenge discrimination at relief agencies in a coalition they called the Joint Conference on Discriminatory Practices. The combined clout of these organizations turned relief agencies into the largest employer of black people in the city. In 1935 the coalition convinced New York's WPA to set explicit nondiscriminatory hiring and promotion policies.

Despite participation in Popular Front activities, though, the majority of African Americans never joined the Communist Party. For a community most sensitive to racial discrimination, the language of class oppression seemed less compelling, particularly because working-class whites themselves rarely spoke of class solidarity across color lines. America's widespread and long-standing distrust of Communism and of the Soviet Union made any public embrace of the party unattractive for a community already finding it difficult to win allies. As Roy Wilkins, civil rights leader and head of the Urban League, later explained, "God knows it was hard enough being black; we certainly didn't need to be red too."[2]

The CP was not the only leftist group to advocate for civil rights. The Socialist Party, slower to see civil rights as a separate issue from economic justice and worker unity, also joined the struggle for black equality in the Depression decade. It too organized committees of the unemployed and held protests and demonstrations focused on black concerns. In Washington, D.C., for example, the Socialist Party publicly cancelled reservations at the hotel hosting its 1933 conference because it refused black guests. In 1937 delegates to the American League Against War and Fascism conference in Pittsburgh picketed segregated facilities there. State and local chapters of Socialist groups routinely protested segregation and racial discrimination. In the pages of progressive journals and at public forums, Socialist leaders demanded stronger antidiscrimination laws and better enforcement of those on the books. The Socialist League for Industrial Democracy and Fellowship of Reconciliation both placed civil rights at the center of their activities.

From its inception in 1932, Highlander Folk School, the Socialist labor-training center in Tennessee, worked with black as well as white workers and organizers; by the next decade it began training civil rights workers for civil disobedience and mass action. In 1936 the Socialist Party created the Workers Defense League (WDL), its own version of the Communist Party's International Labor Defense. The WDL defended the Southern Tenant Farmers' Union; pressed trade unions to pursue more black members; and challenged debt peonage, lynching, and the poll tax. Like the Communists, the Socialists also attracted prominent African Americans from labor leaders A. Philip Randolph and Frank Crosswaith to political activists Bayard Rustin and James Farmer.

Students brought their own forms of activism to the struggle. Both Communist and Socialist youth groups across the country passed resolutions in favor of black civil rights and anti-lynching legislation and in opposition to the poll tax and all forms of segregation. Students at Howard University boycotted local establishments that barred black patrons in 1934. A year later, black and white student leftists in Cleveland succeeded in winning passage of a citywide ordinance against discrimination in any public facility. Each of these protests reveal a black community mobilizing increasingly on its own behalf.

The programs of liberal civil rights groups like the NAACP and Urban League moved leftward in this period in response to Communist and Socialist activity. While those farther to the left often criticized liberal groups as insufficiently militant, significant changes in rhetoric occurred during the Depression that cut across political lines. It was in this decade, for example, that "Uncle Tom" first became a term of derision rather than sympathy. Both Communists and liberals, African Americans and whites, evoked Harriet Beecher Stowe's enslaved hero as a symbol of acquiescence to a degrading and debilitating system. Booker T. Washington came in for public criticism as an Uncle Tom himself. Liberals took up the same issues leftists addressed, with equal vigor. The Urban League, for example, created its own Workers' Councils devoted to educating black workers on economic and trade union issues, passing stronger protections for organizing, and challenging discrimination in the AFL. The NAACP, under the prodding of W. E. B. Du Bois and Abram Harris, moved toward more active engagement with labor issues, taking on employment cases and supporting the creation of Workers' Councils where the Urban League could not do so. Not that the association was entirely happy with Du Bois' economic analysis. He called for greater black economic self-determination in order to build a viable economic and political base for the community. Many criticized him for advocating economic segregation and the leadership pushed him from his editorship of *The Crisis* in 1934.

Incidents of racially and economically motivated violence offered particularly potent opportunities for both liberals and leftists organizing around issues of injustice. Perhaps the most vivid illustration, and certainly the most well known, is the case of the "Scottsboro boys." On March 25, 1931, nine young black men riding a freight train near Scottsboro, Alabama, were arrested for the rape of two white women. Although the charges were false and the prosecution provided no evidence, an all-white court found the defendants guilty and sentenced them to death. While the court was in session, National Guardsmen had to protect the men from angry white mobs.

The gross miscarriage of justice galvanized black and progressive white communities around the country. The NAACP volunteered to provide the men legal counsel for an appeal. The CP's International Labor Defense (ILD) countered that its strategy of combining legal engagement with mass action publicity campaigns would have a greater chance of success. This argument persuaded the convicts' parents and they chose the ILD to handle the cases. The Supreme Court agreed to hear the young men's appeal. In 1932 it ruled in *Powell v. Alabama* that the men had been denied the right to select their own counsel and had therefore been denied the constitutional protection of due process. The case had to be retried.

For four years the ILD fought in the courts and in propaganda campaigns to free the men. Speakers, including the mother of one of the young men, traveled across the country and abroad to publicize the legal travesty. The ILD and Communist Party organized protests and demonstrations and published pamphlets and leaflets linking the case with the larger cause of economic and racial oppression. Thousands of blacks and whites turned out for these rallies or signed petitions demanding justice for the nine men.

In 1935, the Supreme Court moved the case a step further toward resolution when it ruled in *Norris v. Alabama* that the systematic exclusion of black jurors had fatally tainted the trial. Concerned that Alabama would simply find a black Alabama juror and re-indict the men (which is exactly what happened), the ILD shifted tactics and reached out to the NAACP and others to work together in the case. Again, supporters took to the streets, printing presses, meeting halls, and pulpits. Again, community response was overwhelming. Around the world people flocked to hear speakers discuss the case. Black newspapers reported every new development. Hundreds of thousands of letters and petitions reached the ILD, NAACP, the president, Congress, and the governor of Alabama. Finally, in 1937 the coalition Scottsboro Defense Committee convinced the state to drop the charges against four of the men, setting the stage for the eventual pardoning and release of all nine.

Other black victims of the racial justice system were not as fortunate. Lynchings, which had declined slightly in the late 1920s, surged again with economic hardship. Sources vary slightly in the numbers they reported, but one source estimated twenty-one lynchings of black people in 1930, up from seven the year previous. In 1933 that figure rose to twenty-eight, with fifteen in 1934 and twenty in 1935. Many more went unreported. The resurgence in violence reinvigorated the long-standing black campaign for an anti-lynching bill. So long as southern states refused to prosecute such crimes, activists insisted, the only solution was the passage of federal anti-lynching legislation.

The 1930 spike in the number of lynchings prompted Jessie Daniel Ames and the Commission on Interracial Cooperation to organize a group of white women into the Association of Southern Women for the Prevention of Lynching. That they were white women was key to their strategy; the ASWPL mounted a public educational campaign against both lynching and the false claims that such crimes were necessary to protect white womanhood. They also pressed officials and police to act, although they refused to support federal anti-lynching legislation, believing it an inappropriate federal intrusion on states rights. Within a year over 3,000 women had signed on; by 1935 that number had increased to 23,000.

Most political groups concerned about lynching disagreed with the ASWPL and saw federal legislation as the only answer. They too mobilized public opinion, in part through documentation of lynchings, like that of Claude Neal. On October 19, 1934, Neal was arrested in Florida for murder. Authorities sent him to prison in Alabama for his own protection. The attempt failed; a mob broke him out of prison and dragged him back to Florida. There, more than 4,000 whites waited, alerted to the spectacle by announcements in fifteen newspapers. Neal was tortured and then hanged. No police intervened at any point. To arouse public indignation and generate support for an anti-lynching bill, the NAACP published "The Lynching of Claude Neal," a pamphlet that recounted the events, supported by photos and news clippings. The association also circulated petitions of prominent clergy, writers, lawyers, college presidents, and professors in favor of the bill and found congressmen to champion it in both houses. It provided a steady stream of information about lynching and about the bill's progress to Congress, to the president, and to journalists. Organizations from the NCNW to the Communist Party pressed for legislative action as well, lobbying legislators, circulating petitions, publishing their own articles and pamphlets, and holding rallies.

An anti-lynching bill did manage to pass the House, as it had in 1922 and would again in 1940, but failed each time to pass the Senate, with its large number of white-supremacist southern members. Nor did the bill ever receive Roosevelt's open endorsement. Nevertheless, these efforts did have an impact. Between 1917 and 1926, a total of 419 individuals were lynched. In the following decade, the figure dropped to 136. In subsequent years the number of lynchings never exceeded eight, although lynching never ceased as a tool of white supremacist control. The mobilization strategies used by anti-lynching activists, and the local networks they developed, proved invaluable for future organizing.

Black groups' new political aggressiveness was also directed internationally. African Americans, whether oriented to nationalism or integration, had long followed the experiences of black communities around the world. In this decade they coupled such attention with action. When Mussolini invaded Ethiopia in 1935, for example, black churches, fraternal groups, and political organizations launched both protests and relief efforts.

The response to the Ethiopian invasion also reflects another political strategy black activists used in this decade to convince whites of the evils of racism. After Adolph Hitler's Nazi Party gained a powerful foothold in the German Reichstag in 1932, and Hitler himself became chancellor of Germany in 1933, many protests like the one in Norfolk explicitly linked the civil rights struggle at home to the emerging struggle against Fascism abroad. How could a public revolted at Nazi treatment of minority groups accept equally offensive American practices like lynching, segregation, and the exclusion of African Americans from jobs or the ballot box? If it was wrong for Nazis to ban Jews from universities and employment or segregate them in overcrowded and filthy ghettos simply because of their ancestry, similar treatment of black people in the United States was equally wrong. Change the word "Jew" to "Negro" and there was little to distinguish Nazi ideology from that of Jim Crow. The Italian invasion of Ethiopia in 1935 prompted both *Opportunity* and *The Crisis* to point out that the victimization of Africans paralleled that of African Americans. *Kristallnacht*, the 1937 coordinated Nazi attack on German and Austrian Jewish businesses, produced similar observations. The glaring disparity between American condemnation of European discrimination against minorities and America's treatment of its own minorities became increasingly evident and civil rights advocates used it to powerful effect.

Perhaps the most significant political development for advancing African American civil rights was the expansion of legal challenges to segregation and racial discrimination spearheaded by the National Association for the Advancement of Colored People. NAACP lawyers honed their legal strategies and developed an activist cadre of civil rights lawyers in this period, especially through Howard University's law school, strengthened and restructured by Charles Hamilton Houston in 1930 for that purpose. The colleagues he brought into the planning process, including James Nabrit Jr. and William Hastie, would form the core of the NAACP's legal team. The NAACP's new initiatives, while perhaps less public than others' civil rights activities, and certainly less reliant on grass-roots organizing, were nonetheless both innovative and bold.

In 1930 the NAACP and American Fund for Public Service hired Nathan Margold, a white lawyer, to direct a broad-based legal campaign for black equality, beginning with a challenge to segregated education. Although Margold advocated a head-on challenge to the "separate but equal" doctrine of the 1896 *Plessy v. Ferguson* Supreme Court decision, the NAACP opted for a more gradual approach. Since black schools were demonstrably unequal to white, demanding that the requirement of *Plessy* be met—that is, to require rehabilitation and expansion of black educational facilities—would effectively result in bankrupting each state, thus making segregation too expensive for the states to sustain. After a slow start, the legal challenge took off when Houston joined the NAACP legal staff in 1934 along with Hastie and Thurgood Marshall, Houston's student at Howard. Soliciting promising cases, arguing them along consistent lines, educating the public about the democratic injustices of segregation, and crafting carefully argued briefs, the new NAACP legal staff won several significant victories and laid the groundwork for the ultimate challenge of *Plessy*, the 1954 *Brown v. Board of Education* case.

One of its first substantial political victories came in 1930, not through the courts but through the legislature. The NAACP helped convince the Senate to deny President Hoover's candidate, the racist John Parker, a seat on the Supreme Court. While many factors contributed to Parker's failure, the NAACP insisted that the Senate vote demonstrated the emergence of a powerful black political voice. Indeed, many of the pro-Parker and conservative congressional and gubernatorial candidates opposed by the NAACP lost subsequent elections. Frightened, the Republican Party added civil rights planks to its national platform for the first time since 1908. State parties moved to adopt anti-lynching and equal access resolutions.

The strategy of pressing on *Plessy* regarding schools also paid off. Although the University of Maryland began accepting black graduate-school applicants without a court order in 1935, elsewhere legal action was needed to accomplish the same. The Supreme Court ruled in *Missouri ex rel. Gaines v. Canada* (1938), a case brought by the NAACP, that African American Lloyd Gaines could not be excluded from the all-white University of Missouri law school because the state provided no comparable black law school.

In the area of voting rights, the NAACP also won a victory in *Nixon v. Condon* (1932). Texas conducted white-only primary elections, which the court ruled violated the Fifteenth Amendment barring the use of race as a criterion for voting. The victory proved hollow, however, as states across the South simply left it up to the political parties to conduct their own primaries. Since the parties were themselves private entities, exclusion of black voters would not violate the Constitution. The Supreme Court accepted this argument in 1935 in *Grovey v. Townsend*, a loophole that was not plugged until 1944. With these successes, and with the addition of activist new staff including Juanita Jackson Mitchell, Daisy Lampkins, and Ella Baker, the NAACP expanded its membership as well as its portfolio.

All these promising indications of growing community activism in the 1930s also produced new groups and coalitions eager to expand African Americans' potential strength. Mary McLeod Bethune, lamenting the caution of the National Association of Colored Women, organized the National Council of Negro Women (NCNW) in 1935. Devoting itself to removing barriers to sexual and racial advancement, and frequently working in coalitions with other black and women's organizations, the explicitly politically minded NCNW quickly grew to twenty affiliates and ninety locals around the country. The 1935 conference of the Joint Committee on National Recovery, "The Position of the Negro in the Present Economic Crisis," that criticized the inadequacy of current New Deal policies also called for greater joint planning and action to further black interests.

In response to that call, John Davis of the Joint Committee on National Recovery formed the National Negro Congress (NNC) in 1935 to be a coordinating body for civil rights action. Attracting more than 550 black civic, political, and fraternal organizations to its first annual meeting in 1936, the NNC pledged its member agencies to advance African Americans' social, economic, and political rights. Under the leadership of A. Philip Randolph, the NNC organized local councils and launched a series of political projects. It held demonstrations around the country on behalf of anti-lynching legislation, fought (unsuccessfully) for the inclusion of agricultural and domestic workers under Social Security and labor protections, and supported progressive candidates in local and state elections. Its breadth of outreach, however, proved its weakness as well as its strength. Communist groups' inclusion frightened and alienated more moderate black voices and within a few years most of the NNC's base was gone. Nevertheless its brief flowering provided a crucial foundation for collaboration among African American groups committed to the advancement of the race, and it offered a model of the power that a united black movement for civil rights could wield.

Among the most successful examples of urban grassroots political organizing during the decade of the Great Depression were the "Don't Buy Where You Can't Work" campaigns, named for the signs protesters carried as they marched in front of offending stores. The reality of continued economic hardship and racial discrimination in hiring prompted African American protests in cities across the country, North and South. These and similar efforts helped spur community organizing on a variety of issues in many cities and towns, experimenting with new political tactics to challenge, if not to end, economic hardship and racial discrimination.

Most of the business owners in black communities, both black and white, were themselves poor or had escaped poverty only through their entrepreneurial activities. Poorly capitalized and small, these shops often survived only by using family members as employees and keeping expenses to a minimum. Because these stores were unable to purchase in bulk, goods cost more, and those costs were passed on to customers. Prices for food or clothing were therefore higher in these neighborhoods, despite—in fact largely because of—the poverty of its residents. These imbalances had all existed before the Depression, but the economic collapse worsened the situation. Desperate families pleaded with storeowners for credit and cut their purchasing. Many customers were forced to default on their debts and storeowners had little recourse. Thousands of businesses, especially those that were smaller and undercapitalized, went bankrupt. Not surprisingly, a high proportion of these were African American.

Those that managed to hang on, both black and white, did so by restricting credit or increasing credit prices and limiting their workforce. Some kept prices low by stocking less expensive, poor-quality goods. They may have been doing only what they believed they needed to do to survive, but from the residents' point of view the situation appeared rather different. Shopkeepers sold shoddy goods at inflated prices, took advantage of the needy, treated their clients poorly, and refused to hire area residents. Many resented black storeowners for such practices, but they expressed greater anger at whites, who not only took economic advantage of customers, but who also discriminated against local residents in their hiring practices. If white merchants did seek workers, family connections and racism combined to ensure that most hired from outside the black community, particularly for clerical jobs. While all employment discrimination was insulting and economically hurtful, discrimination by white shopkeepers who operated in black neighborhoods seemed particularly odious. Despite making money in the community, these storeowners gave nothing back in the form of employment. Those who did take on black workers usually limited them to the least skilled and worst paying jobs. It is hardly surprising, then, that black residents in many cities, North and South, organized protests.

Many of these protests took nationalist forms, insisting that black people should support their own. "Buy black" campaigns, often sponsored by local black storeowners, gained ground in numerous cities and towns with large black populations, including Chicago, Richmond, Baltimore, Detroit, Philadelphia, and New York. The *Pittsburgh Courier* argued that keeping more money within the black community would help support local black institutions like churches and schools. Some historians have argued these merchants' motives were more economic than ideological; anything that might bolster trade at their stores was worth embracing. Whatever the truth, and it presumably varied from individual to individual, many in the black community employed the nationalist rhetoric of Marcus Garvey and the Universal Negro Improvement Association during the difficult days of the Depression.

Others, often in the same cities, fought to compel white storeowners to hire more black clerks and other workers. They launched boycotts of offending stores and organized picket lines publicizing the group's demands. The boycotts and media publicity often had an immediate impact, and the strategy spread across the country, from Durham to Chicago, Seattle to St. Louis, Cleveland to New York, Detroit to Washington, D.C. These protests drew the support of many black political organizations, from the National Council of Negro Women to the NAACP. Occasionally these efforts received cooperation from white organizations like the South Central Association, a group of Chicago Jewish business owners. Under pressure from the Anti-Defamation League, the SCA agreed to increase the hiring of black clerks, contribute to neighborhood programs, and monitor the business practices of its members.

Some of the earliest employment campaigns were sponsored by the Urban League, which launched boycotts in St. Louis and Chicago in 1929. When *Chicago Whip* editor Joseph Bibb spoke of that city's successful campaign, he inspired the Harlem Housewives League to initiate a similar drive a year later. The Harlem group had only limited success, but it did in turn inspire others to form Housewives Leagues in their own cities including Durham, Baltimore, Washington, D.C., and Cleveland.

These leagues sought to combine the purchasing power of women with economic nationalism to press for better hiring policies by local white stores, occasionally even those outside of black neighborhoods. Detroit's Housewives League, which claimed 10,000 members in 1934, helped lead protests in that city that succeeded in integrating the workforce of a supermarket chain. Elsewhere local groups combined to initiate their own protests or support those already in progress. In Washington, D.C., a coalition of activists that included Mary McLeod Bethune, William Hastie, and Thurgood Marshall called themselves the New Negro Alliance. The *St. Louis Argus* advocated for protesters in that city. The North Philadelphia Civic Club, an organization of churches and social service groups, provided support to Philadelphia's "Don't Buy" campaign. In New York, several groups, ranging from nationalist to Communist, competed for leadership of the movement.

Politically active black ministers participated in, or even led, "Don't Buy" campaigns in many cities and brought their congregations with them. But in many places, women were the primary organizers. Virtually everywhere they provided the majority of picketers. Socialists and Communists generally also supported these protests, so long as the hiring of black workers did not require the firing of whites. Middle-class workers with skills were most likely to benefit from these campaigns, although the opening of previously white-only jobs improved opportunities for the working class as well. Not surprisingly, therefore, these coalitions generally enjoyed broad support in black communities.

Even criminals faced demands to integrate their operations. When white mobster Dutch Schultz took over the numbers game in Harlem in 1932, the community refused to purchase numbers (place bets) in his stores unless he hired black clerks to staff them and black runners to bring bets to collection points and distribute winnings. He capitulated under the pressure. The success of this boycott showed as much as any other the power of black consumers.

Many of these protests provoked strong white response. Not only did white storekeepers counter that they could not afford to hire any more workers, that African Americans did not have the needed skills, or that black clerks would alienate white customers, they also complained that the entrances to their establishments were blocked or their customers threatened. A few alleged that protesters had been violent or threatening. In 1934 a group of white Harlem shopkeepers went to court. They argued that the picket lines of the Citizens League for Fair Play, a coalition of eighteen churches and forty-four other organizations, were illegal. The court agreed and issued an injunction prohibiting the protests on the grounds that they were only legal in cases of employee grievances. Since picketers were not employees, their protest had no legal standing and therefore enjoyed no legal protection. When the state courts upheld the injunctions, protesters faced the choice of disbanding or breaking the law. Such injunctions quickly followed elsewhere.

Most protestors elected to follow the law and returned to quieter, behind-the-scenes strategies despite their limited effectiveness. Some, however, particularly nationalist activists like Sufi Abdul Hamid, continued to stage public protests, enduring arrests and harassment as a result. Hamid, who began his political career in Chicago and ended it in Harlem, complained that even when white employers hired African American workers, they chose only the lightest skinned among them. Among these nationalists' most ardent supporters were West Indians, generally dark skinned and more familiar with employers' preferences for black people of lighter color. Such allegations had a basis in fact. Status based on color was widespread in the black as well as the white community, with lighter skin supposedly a mark of greater quality and attractiveness. Hamid and others called attention to this fact, linking class and race in a different way than their more law-abiding counterparts.

But these protests rarely succeeded either, as they were opposed not only by whites and police but often by black leaders of the earlier coalitions, who saw these protests as threats to the broader struggle as well as to their own leadership. After the picket lines evaporated, employers reneged on their promises and no new positions opened. The "Don't Buy" campaigns, like so many other political efforts, seemed to have been a complete failure. The hopes of thousands who had picketed and protested appeared once again dashed.

In 1935 Harlem residents erupted in a riot, sparked when a local white storeowner accused a young boy of shoplifting and called police. False rumors of police brutality combined with smoldering black resentment at shopkeepers and police, and thousands poured into the streets. The angry protest became a full-blown riot, causing dozens of injuries and hundreds of thousands of dollars of damage. A commission established by Mayor Fiorello La Guardia to examine the riot's causes concluded that it was provoked by widespread community frustration at, among other things, its continued exploitation at the hands of white businesses.

In 1938 the Supreme Court removed the legal impediments to all the "Don't Buy" protests by ruling in favor of the Washington, D.C., protests in *New Negro Alliance v. Sanitary Grocery Co.* The court found that hiring grievances involving race were legitimate labor issues under the 1935 Labor Relations Act. Therefore, the justices ruled, protests and pickets demanding the hiring of black workers enjoyed the same protections that union organizing did. This decision opened the way for renewed protests around the nation. Now even larger coalitions organized picket lines and demonstrations, bringing in church congregations, political leaders, and self-help groups. Often they extended their protests to union and municipal hiring as well. In Seattle, black leaders fought to integrate Boeing, the city's largest employer. In New York, the Greater New York Coordinating Committee for Employment, sponsored by 200 organizations representing 170,000 members, negotiated hiring agreements with the Uptown Chamber of Commerce, the telephone, electric, and gas companies, the 1939 World's Fair, and a bus company. One of its leaders, Adam Clayton Powell Jr., used these successes as his springboard to a legislative career. D.C.'s New Negro Alliance reported that more than 5,000 new jobs had opened to black workers in more than fifty stores around the city. Meanwhile its lawyers, including James Nabrit Jr., and Thurgood Marshall, joined the NAACP as staff attorneys where they continued their struggles against discrimination.

The legacy of these employment protests was even more significant than improved hiring practices, electoral successes, or helpful court decisions. The strategies employed by these coalitions, ranging from protests and publicity to mass pickets and boycotts, provided models for the civil rights movement of the 1950s and 1960s. Despite their poverty, mobilized and unified black consumers held substantial clout. The skills gained in organizing coalitions among groups who generally disagreed or competed with each other also proved crucial to the civil rights movement. The arguments, based on ethics and justice but rooted as well in economics, provided effective rhetorical pressure points from which to organize. Along with the other protest movements of the Depression, employment-based protests provided a base for future political struggles for civil rights.

In the end, the products of Depression-era black organizing were primarily hope and momentum. Spurred by the hardships of the Depression, the promises of the New Deal and the unfairness of continued discrimination, African Americans worked on both the local and national level to improve their lives. They revitalized existing organizations and created new ones, fighting for equal access to the ballot, fair treatment on the shop floor, better educational opportunities, equitable government aid, and greater political representation. Working separately or in coalition with other black and multiracial groups, black leaders and the organizations that backed them used all the tools at their disposal—boycotts, protests, negotiation, legal challenges, electoral pressure, legislative lobbying, pickets, and more—to achieve their goals. In the Depression decade, few of these efforts succeeded fully. Neither liberals nor leftists transformed race relations. They brought small advances to black electoral clout and some improvements to local black communities, but they could not substantively alter the balance of power. Their greatest contribution was in the groundwork of tactics and community organizing they laid, groundwork later political movements would build upon. These activists gained crucial skills and political sophistication and inspired the community to continue the fight. By demonstrating the potential for protest that lurked beneath even the quietest of black communities, these protests represented the early stirrings of the civil rights movement. For the moment, most protests remained polite. That would not be true forever. The political, legal, and legislative successes of national groups and local coalitions organized around economic justice, limited though they may have been, bolstered black support for both mainstream and leftist political action that would expand into a mass movement that would change the nation.

Notes

1. Editorial, *Pittsburgh Courier*, September 11, 1932.
2. Roy Wilkins, *Standing Fast: The Autobiography of Roy Wilkins* (New York: Penguin Books, 1994), 210, referring to the period around 1950.

~

CHAPTER FIVE

Weary Blues: Black Communities and Black Culture

Black community life could not remain unaffected in light of Depression-era changes in opportunity. Increased poverty meant more hunger, more over-crowding, more illness, more pressure on families. Black community organizations mobilized to aid the desperate in their community, providing what aid and services they could. Many self-help or "uplift" groups had been doing so for decades, but the Depression pressed them to even greater efforts. Others formed or refocused their energies to meet the growing need. Black migration rose again as the poor took to the road to find greater opportunities or to share costs with family members or friends elsewhere. This intensified the pressure on black communities and support services. Continued white resistance meant newcomers squeezed into existing black neighborhoods that were often in poor physical condition and lacking in social services.

But migrants also brought new energy with them. Their different experiences and styles combined in these black enclaves to create and reshape vibrant social spaces. Although physically most of these black neighborhoods were ghettos, socially they were communities in which black political, artistic, and intellectual expression could flourish alongside the growing political activism. At the same time the greater visibility of black leaders and greater attention government paid to black communities offered more African Americans a public platform than ever before. Long before the Depression, of course, black intellectuals, artists, politicians, performers, and athletes had gained recognition for their contributions to American life and culture. The 1930s increased that recognition, especially as New Deal programs provided new spaces for the training and showcasing of a new generation. Their achievements helped shape new views of race relations and fostered an ever-increasing sense of black pride.

These two components of black life, art and community, cannot be separated. In fundamental ways, black communal life shaped black cultural and artistic production. Artists used the black cultural styles and social and emotional connections they grew up with to interpret their lives and communicate their experiences. At the same time, art provided an outlet for the pains, frustrations, joys, and triumphs so deeply intertwined in black lives. As Richard Wright put it in *Twelve Million Black Voices*:

> Our music makes the whole world dance. . . . But only a few of those who dance and sing with us suspect the rawness of life out of which our laughing-crying tunes and quick dance steps come; they do not know that our songs and dances are our banner of hope flung desperately up in the face of a world that has pushed us to the wall.[1]

Despite the infusion of government aid and employment, living conditions in the Depression decade remained harsh for the vast majority of African Americans, North and South, urban and rural. While few starved, few prospered. Most families saw their living standards plummet; they moved to less expensive housing or moved in with friends or family, bought the least expensive food, and went without new clothing and other necessities. Their need had hit crisis proportions. What did life look like under these conditions?

A 1935–1936 National Consumer Purchases Study of the rural South, where so many African Americans still lived, found that more than 80 percent of black farm families and half of white lived in homes rated as "poor." Federal relief agencies documented families living in precarious, tumbledown shacks with rotting floors, their flimsy walls lined with newspapers to keep the wind from whistling through. Many lacked furniture; in most of these homes beds, tables, and chairs were makeshift. Virtually all these shacks lacked running water, electricity, or telephones. Front yards of dust and dirt intersected unpaved roads.

These families earned so little that it is a wonder they survived at all. Many barely did. Hunting or small gardens supplemented wages, but not enough to meet even the minimum level government agencies estimated as necessary for subsistence. Unable to afford adequate food or health and sanitary supplies, health suffered. What health care there was in rural towns was provided on a segregated basis, if at all. Rural southern black children were smaller and sicker than their white neighbors, and they and their parents

The Federal Housing Authority completely rebuilt St. Thomas Street in New Orleans, one of thousands such renovations. Here we see photos of the block before and after the U.S. Housing Authority came through in 1940. Courtesy of the Franklin D. Roosevelt Library Digital Archives.

routinely went without any health or dental care. Malnutrition, lice, pellagra, and dysentery were widespread. Tuberculosis, malaria, worms, rickets, even typhoid devastated these families.

Housing in urban areas, North or South, proved little better. The 1934 National Housing Act established a Federal Housing Administration (FHA) to expand housing and aid the building industry. The Supreme Court had overturned racial zoning laws in 1917, but such practices remained commonplace. Until 1948 when the Supreme Court declared the agreements unenforceable, residents of many neighborhoods signed restrictive housing covenants, promising not to sell or rent their property to specific groups, a changing list that virtually always included African Americans and Jews.

In support of such widespread segregation practices, the FHA's *Underwriting Manual* warned that integrating neighborhoods led to the decline of property values, and the agency refused mortgages to any black families seeking to move into white neighborhoods. As usual, federal administrators explained they did so because they feared antagonizing southern white officials. They claimed they were realists, protecting homeowners from the falling prices that would result if neighborhoods changed. But the impact on residential segregation was substantial. It wrote into policy existing racist practices, which had the effect of extending and solidifying the separation of white and black living areas and intensifying overcrowding and rental exploitation in existing black neighborhoods. The available housing stock was already poorer in black neighborhoods than elsewhere. FHA housing policies therefore froze that pattern in place, forcing newcomers to squeeze in among existing tenants or homeowners in already marginal areas of town. There was greater overcrowding than ever in Birmingham's Tuxedo Junction, Chicago's South Side, New York's Harlem, Dallas's Oak Cliff, and other poor neighborhoods.

Meanwhile unscrupulous building owners, recognizing that their tenants had few options, raised rents with impunity. While rents fell in the 1930s along with other prices, the costs in black areas remained higher than equally poor white areas. To take New York as an example, during the early years of the Depression the average Harlem resident paid almost double what equally poor Italians in East Harlem paid. By mid-decade, costs in both areas had dropped, although black Harlem's rents remained higher—and higher than the rental support provided by any relief agency. Meanwhile, among the 8,300 poor families the Charity Organization Society aided in 1935, black family earnings had dropped to almost half of their already low 1929 pay. White families' earnings had also declined but by far less. As a consequence, while poor whites' housing costs amounted to approximately a quarter of their income, black families spent more than half of their entire earnings on rent.

Overcrowding in black neighborhoods therefore worsened still more, as strapped families took in boarders rather than face eviction for failure to pay rent. Even new housing projects, which represented far greater governmental investment in black housing than ever before and offered substantially higher quality living space, were received with some ambivalence by black community leaders because they reinforced the residential segregation patterns that had helped turn black areas into ghettos. Again to take New York as the example, the Harlem River Houses, built well within the confines of the black neighborhood, offered 574 good quality apartments for nineteen to thirty-one dollars a month in rent. More than 20,000 families applied for those spots. They might not be able to escape the ghetto, and indeed many preferred not to live isolated among whites, but they could at least hope to live more decently within it.

The proportion of apartments labeled "unfit" or "substandard" by relief and housing officials during the Depression was vastly greater in these segregated black neighborhoods, despite their high rents. In Savannah, Georgia, over half of all apartments occupied by black families were considered unfit or in need of major repairs, compared with just over 10 percent occupied by whites. In Norfolk, four times as many black renters as white lived in such "unfit" conditions. Twice as many African American as white renters lacked indoor toilets. In Atlanta's Beaver Slide neighborhood, 80 percent of all apartments required major repairs or were judged unfit for human habitation; in Dallas that figure was 86 percent. Across the country, approximately one-fourth of black families earning less than $1,000 a year lived in buildings without private toilets—double the proportion of comparable white families. In Houston and Richmond, poor black neighborhoods had no paved streets; a third of all Birmingham black families had no running water.

Northern cities offered little better. In Pittsburgh, almost 60 percent of black apartments had no toilets. In Detroit, 34 percent of black units needed major repairs or were unfit for habitation, compared with 6 percent of white. One-third of Cleveland's black community lived in similarly "unfit" conditions. In Chicago, Cleveland, Detroit, and Harlem housing inspectors reported families crammed into windowless basements or squatting in condemned buildings. Hall toilets, rats, poor ventilation, landlord negligence, and other physical challenges joined the poverty and overcrowding to create too many unlivable spaces in which too many black people were nonetheless forced to live. The opening scene of *Native Son*, Richard Wright's searing portrait of a black Chicago teen destroyed by such degrading and limiting circumstances, depicts rats running across the apartment and under the feet of the protagonist's petrified baby sister.

In the vicious cycle of politics, poorer neighborhoods with less clout received fewer municipal services, which worsened conditions still further. The ratio of hospital beds, school classrooms, and playground spaces to residents were all far worse in poor black neighborhoods than in better-off and white areas, and the number of residents per square acre was higher. Harlem had the highest population density of any neighborhood in all of New York City, but its proportion of parks and playgrounds came to only a quarter of the city's average. Racism played a further role in the decline of black areas, because even in the North many private social services refused to serve black people.

As a result of poverty, overcrowding, and discrimination in the provision of services, black people's health suffered in urban as well as rural areas. In the United States as a whole, there was one hospital bed for every 139 white people in 1928, compared with one for every 1,941 black people. Although health spending increased with the New Deal, such racial disparities changed little. In fact, the number of black hospitals nationwide actually fell. By the end of the Depression there were only 79 black hospitals in the South, and 124 in the entire country. Overall, death rates for both races did decline, thanks primarily to New Deal programs that extended health care and the ability to pay for it to a greater number of needy individuals. But although the mortality rate per thousand in the African American community dropped dramatically in the 1930s, it still lagged well beyond white. Demographers express these figures in terms of expected life spans. They estimated that a black child born in 1940 could expect to live to age fifty-two if she were female, and age forty-nine if he were male. For whites both figures were substantially higher: sixty-five and sixty-one years respectively.

Racist southern health services explain much of this racial discrepancy. While in the North and West black people could receive care in any public hospital, that was rarely the case in the South. Those southern white hospitals that did serve black patients placed them in segregated wards, which were often in the basement or other poorly ventilated areas and inadequately staffed. Some did not even separate contagious black patients from others. Some southern black patients did have access to white doctors, who typically served them only on specific days. Most of the close to 10 million black people living in the South, however, relied on the approximately 1,700 black doctors and 500 black public health nurses, the majority of whom worked in cities. That included 90 percent of North Carolina's black doctors, for example, despite the overwhelmingly rural black population there.

While virtually all northern babies were born attended by physicians, in the South in 1937 that figure was 90 percent for white babies but only 35 percent for black. Comparing death rates by race in southern cities in 1930 reveals a higher black than white death rate in every single large southern city, as well as across the South as a whole. In Atlanta the death rate was more than twice as high for black as for white residents, as it was in Birmingham, Charlotte, Chattanooga, Dallas, Houston, Jacksonville, Norfolk, and Savannah.

But the racial inequities in health and mortality transcended region. In Chicago, the Public Health Service reported that the death rate from tuberculosis (TB) in the period between 1939 and 1941 was more than five times higher for African Americans than whites. In Los Angeles the ratio of black TB deaths to white was almost three to one. In Detroit the ratio approached six to one. In every city mortality and morbidity (illness) rates in black areas exceeded those in neighborhoods inhabited by whites.

One of the most notorious abuses of health care in the United States also began during the Depression years, when the U.S. Health Service decided to study syphilis, a sexually transmitted disease. Scientists had good reason to do so: when untreated, syphilis led to significant health problems, in some cases even to paralysis and heart failure. Doctors and nurses in Tuskegee recruited 622 poor black male sharecroppers living nearby to participate in a syphilis study. Two-thirds of these men had the disease; the rest were disease-free and used as controls. The study promised free health care and treatment but instead, and without the men's knowledge or consent, for close to forty years doctors and nurses gave the infected men sugar pills, conducted invasive and painful examinations to study the course of the disease, and autopsied them when they died. The public and the surviving men did not learn of the horrifying deception until a newspaper broke the story in 1972. To some, at least, black people remained little above laboratory rats. Regarding every single aspect of health care, race still mattered.

African Americans did make substantial gains in education, where the New Deal had a dramatic effect. More than a million African Americans attended classes funded by various New Deal programs, with the result that the overall illiteracy rate of the black population dropped 10 percent in a single decade. In southern black schools the length of the school year, teacher salaries, and the numbers of African American young people enrolled all increased during the 1930s. The number of black children completing high school rose from 17 to 30 percent and many more had access to vocational training than ever before.

Despite these advances, many different indicators suggested the glass remained half empty. By the end of the decade, southern black teachers still earned half of what white teachers did and fewer black than white pupils graduated from high school or attended college. A 1939 study of southern black education consistently found lower numbers of black children enrolled in schools despite compulsory education laws, shorter school years for those children, poorer transportation services to school, far higher student-teacher ratios, and salaries for black teachers that often did not even reach a subsistence wage. The report lamented the shamefully inadequate condition of black school buildings and lack of supplies, offering a student's description of an East Texas school as a typical example:

> The building was a crude box shack built by the Negroes out of old slabs and scrap lumber. Windows and doors were badly broken. The floor was in such condition that one had to walk carefully to keep from going through cracks and weak boards. Daylight was easily visible through walls, floor and roof. . . . Its only equipment consisted of a few roughhewn seats, an old stove brought from a junk pile, a crude homemade pulpit, a very small table, and a large water barrel. . . . There was no blackboard and . . . no desks. . . . Fifty-two children were enrolled. All these crowded into a single small room, with benches for but half the number. The teacher and pupils had tacked newspapers on the walls to keep the wind out. Rain poured through the roof, and school was dismissed when it rained. No supplies, except a broom, were furnished the school by the district during the year.[2]

White southern rural schools also tended to fall far below desired standards, but in every case black schools proved far worse. Even after twenty years of Rosenwald Fund aid for black school construction, totaling more than $28 million, the total per-student value of black school property in 1936 was approximately one-fifth that of white. Although the racial disparities in educational spending had declined somewhat since the 1920s, Mississippi, Georgia, and South Carolina still spent five times as much on each white child for secondary education as they did on black.

As a result, few southern black students managed to attend college. Nonetheless, because the National Youth Administration allocated scholarships more equitably than most other New Deal programs, opportunities for black higher education were better than they would otherwise have been. Fully 15 percent of all students attending southern land-grant colleges were black. However, black colleges received only 9 percent of state and federal funds. Put slightly differently, for each dollar a southern white college received for a student in 1936, a black college received fifty-nine cents. As a result most black colleges were underfunded and at the same time confronted students who had been poorly served by their earlier schooling. For most, it was all they could do to cover the basics. Although there were 117 black colleges in the South, a 1939 report found that only 5 private black colleges could offer advanced work.

All this mattered because educational level helped determine economic opportunity. Of course the professions required advanced schooling. But even skilled work by and large required greater education. The median education of black male skilled workers in 1936 was 8.4 years, higher than the southern black average. Additionally, those who reported holding skilled jobs from 1930 to 1936 averaged more education than those who did not.

Northern schools were legally integrated, but, unsurprisingly, local schools in black neighborhoods generally proved more crowded and more run-down, offering fewer services and a more limited selection of courses. Sometimes concerted black protest increased funds for a specific school or convinced local officials to improve facilities with New Deal funds. By and large, though, northern black schools remained virtually as segregated as those in the South and the quality of education poorer than in nearby, wealthier districts.

Despite New Deal programs, then, conditions for most African Americans remained dreadful. The Depression proved so severe, and racial discrimination so resistant to change, that government aid and community activism could not overcome them. A 1940 White House Conference on Children drew the same conclusion, lamenting the inadequacy of public services in black communities, their poorer schools and health care, higher rents, and lack of opportunity.

Responding to the desperate need, black neighbors and communities rallied together to help. Well before the 1930s, black communities had organized to ease hardship among their members. But the urgency brought on by the Depression spurred even greater self-help efforts by black groups ranging from women's clubs to church congregations. It was in local communities that black organizations often made the difference between survival and devastation. In Norfolk, Virginia, for example, a coalition of black social welfare, religious, and labor groups began to coordinate aid and support for the poor as early as 1928. Around the nation, black churches, large and small, urban and rural, supported unemployed parishioners and other impoverished families in the community. They served hundreds of free meals a day and provided clothing, food, and money to the needy and unemployed. Some were even able to offer jobs.

Especially in urban areas where many congregations worshiped side by side, they often combined forces to expand their reach. Prominent ministers from seventeen black New York churches organized the Harlem Cooperating Committee on Relief and Unemployment in 1930. Calling for donations from all working adults in Harlem, the committee helped 20,000 black residents with food, clothing, rent, and other aid in its first seven months. At the same time it fed approximately 2,400 people a day. Even tiny storefronts did their share. The emergency touched everyone.

Black club women and other self-help activists provided their own aid, including shelter, food, job training, and educational programs. They had long provided such services, primarily to urban newcomers. Now, they expanded to accommodate the greater need. A Chicago women's club provided residential space for seventeen homeless women. The Sojourner Truth Home in Seattle housed single women. Others provided day care centers and after-school programs like Harlem's Hope Day Nursery for Colored Children and Utopia Children's House, which provided warm meals as well as education and recreation for hungry neighborhood youngsters. Black groups organized food and clothing drives, bought supplies for economically strapped schools, and ran health clinics. Residential and support services expanded to serve the increasing number of children orphaned or relinquished by desperate families who were unable to care for them.

The National Urban League, Phelps-Stokes Fund, YWCA, and other multiracial national service agencies also combined direct financial aid to the poor with the provision of social services. Like all-black groups they expanded their welfare, health, and education programs to meet the crisis. They worked with local hospitals and doctors to provide health and nutrition services; funded educational and social service programs; and established safe, affordable residences for newcomers while expanding the employment, educational, and recreational services their missions required.

Given the economic catastrophe, these groups pressed especially hard to improve employment opportunities for black workers. The NAACP threatened lawsuits against municipal hospitals in northern cities that did not hire black doctors or nurses. The NUL established new employment agencies to match employers with employees and negotiated with businesses to hire trained African American workers at their skill level. For the first time, the league also succeeded in becoming a beneficiary of Community Chests, municipal fund-raising campaigns whose proceeds were divided among a coalition of local charitable agencies. This new money enabled local Urban League branches to provide still more services to the needy.

Self-help efforts, while not enough to solve the desperate poverty of the unemployed, saved hundreds of thousands from starvation and despair. But the already high level of need also limited these organizations' ability to challenge or remedy the structural problems that lay beneath that need. They had to devote what money and resources they had to meet the immediate crisis. The launching of New Deal agencies changed that. Now these local groups also organized politically. Not only had fund raising among poor individuals proven excruciatingly limited, but the New Deal's responsiveness to black leaders had demonstrated that political pressure produced results. A coalition of black benevolent organizations in Norfolk pressed the city to hire black workers for civic building projects. Seattle's Phyllis Wheatley YWCA expanded its community services to include the hosting of political protest meetings. Across the country, Urban League chapters met with government relief agencies as well as private businesses to facilitate the hiring of black workers. Local churches provided space for rallies to protest employment discrimination. Their congregations lobbied civic leaders and marched on City Hall to demand equitable aid for the black poor. Children's aid groups demanded more municipal services. Even local branches of the Communist Party and Garvey's Universal Negro Improvement Association aided constituents in obtaining government relief. Unemployed councils agitated for higher relief allowances amid their broader protests against the exploitative capitalist government that provided them. Although the UNIA continued to advocate for immigration to Africa and for black unity and separatism, it also set up local offices where the black unemployed could come and receive help in filling out the complex residency and relief application forms. In New York, UNIA members met with families whose petitions for relief had been rejected, helped them collect necessary information, and even accompanied them to relief offices. The Communist Party did the same in Birmingham. This direct engagement with government programs reinforced the lessons the economic, electoral, and civic improvement campaigns of the 1930s had taught: external resources came more readily to an effectively mobilized black community.

Surviving the Depression was emotional as well as physical, and African Americans created and reshaped their communal life in response to the struggles they faced. Many looked to religious communities for spiritual as well as physical relief, and urban black church congregations grew with the population. Many found they had to hold multiple services on Sundays, all to overflow crowds, in order to accommodate their members. The largest black denominations remained African Methodist Episcopal (AME), AME Zion, and Baptist, but hundreds of smaller congregations, denominations, and sects flourished as well, including black Catholics, black Jews, and black Muslims.

Every town and city had groups of worshipers who had followed individual preachers into former storefronts. New religious figures attracted followers as well. These included Bishop Charles Manuel "Sweet Daddy" Grace, who founded the United House of Prayer for All People of the Church on the Rock of the Apostolic Faith. His racially integrated, revival-style services included brass bands, public baptisms, and speaking in tongues. The pageantry of his services, the energy of his preaching, and the deeply Christian, patriotic images he evoked attracted thousands looking for both hope and diversion, and his followers established branches in more than twenty cities. Blending the economic with the spiritual, he also marketed a line of soaps, powders, coffees, and teas that his supporters believed had healing properties.

Similarly compelling and similarly spiritually entrepreneurial was Father Divine. Born George Baker, Divine implied, but never directly stated, that he was God. He preached love, peace, and community without regard to race. Bands of his followers, "angels," lived together in "Heavens" and pooled their resources for the common good. Father Divine provided sumptuous banquets in these Heavens and sold full meals at Divine restaurants for fifteen cents. His Peace Missions expanded from his starting place in New York into numerous other cities in the Northeast and even in a few foreign countries. At the movement's height, 150 Peace Missions served Divine's followers. Black religious communities proved as diverse as black politics. Some ministers spoke of the world to come, while others demanded greater justice in this one. Some advocated quiet endurance, others embraced protest. Although most ministers tried to help their congregants obtain aid, others like Father Divine prohibited their followers from accepting any private or public relief.

While Divine preached that race was a fiction, black nationalism also found religious expression during the Depression. The Nation of Islam (NOI), founded in Detroit in 1930 by W. D. Fard, emphasized black self-sufficiency and racial separatism. While the NOI incorporated many of the universalist ideas of traditional Islam, it focused on those dispersed from Africa, arguing, along with Marcus Garvey and Noble Drew Ali, that they had a particular destiny to fulfill. Four years after its founding Fard mysteriously disappeared, and Elijah Muhammad (born Elijah Poole) succeeded him. The Nation continued growing through the 1930s. It was declining by the late 1950s when a young convert named Malcolm X took a position in a Harlem Temple and reenergized the movement.

Black churches certainly provided community, but then, so did hardship itself. Rural and urban black families and communities expanded on time-honored practices of barter and mutual aid to help them through difficult times. A woman cooking vegetables might ask to borrow oil or beans from a neighbor. A third might contribute bread or even a little meat for a communal supper. Women dressed one another's hair in exchange for tending their children while they worked, or shared clothing or household tools. Workers pooled money for celebrations or to aid sick co-workers. Families took in relatives and friends, sometimes whole families, who had lost their homes. Married children returned home to live if they could not find work. There is some evidence that more men deserted their families during the Depression than before or after, because of their inability to support them, but if true, the numbers stabilized by the end of the decade. In both 1930 and 1940, two-thirds of black men older than fifteen and three-fourths of black women were married. While hardship might reshuffle living arrangements, family commitments by and large remained intact.

Rural families hunted, fished, and planted small gardens to supplement meager earnings, sharing rides to town to save on gas. Even in cities, some planted vegetable gardens in deserted lots. Others held parties to raise money for rent; neighbors and friends paid an admission fee and enjoyed food, music, and dancing. Black jazz musicians reported having two musical lives—performances in clubs frequented by white patrons and afterhours sessions at these "rent parties" where they were free to improvise and enjoy the company of black friends and fellow musicians.

Like rent parties, much of black communal life provided both a respite from worry and an opportunity for black employment. Most famous were Harlem clubs like the Apollo or Savoy Ballroom, but no black community, rural or urban, was without at least one gathering place. Dance halls, bars, restaurants, and nightclubs dotted black communities, often hosting black entertainers and providing social space for young people. Hotels served those passing through; often their bars or dance floors drew locals as well. Detroiters enjoyed the Chocolate Bar and Forest Club and dozens of other hot spots. Los Angeles had Central Avenue, with the Kentucky Club and Lincoln Theater. Kansas City offered Lucille's Paradise, Chez Paree, and others near the famed corner of Eighteenth and Vine. Atlanta's Decatur Street and Memphis's Beale Street were crowded with clubs of their own. Some of these nightclubs attracted white patrons, eager to hear jazz and blues, but most offered all-black social spaces where residents could relax, away from white eyes. Theaters in black communities offered venues for politically charged as well as classic dramas. Many black playwrights staged their first productions there, often with New Deal funding. They hosted vaudeville comedians and black repertory companies, staged Federal Theatre Project performances and educated audiences through Living Newspapers. Black singers like Marian Anderson and Paul Robeson performed on these stages as well.

Illegal activities contributed to black community life in their own way. Prostitution, both black and white, remained an unfortunate staple of poor black communities, and bootlegging persisted even after Prohibition ended. Even more widespread were large-scale gambling games called "numbers" or "policy." Individuals placed bets as to what numbers would appear in the newspaper on a given day. Usually stock sales or sports scores determined the winning numbers. The formula varied from city to city, but the bets operated like a lottery, with winners taking a proportion of the betting pool. Playing the numbers had begun in the nineteenth century, but it expanded in this desperate time, particularly in poor communities. Cities with large black populations often sustained several competing games simultaneously. Thousands played the numbers, and hundreds more made their living from it. Shopkeepers and bar owners profited from the celebrations of the winners; stores that served as fronts for numbers games did their own brisk business; and go-betweens, or runners, who collected bets and distributed winnings, earned a portion of the profits. This explains the pressure Harlemites put on underworld figure Dutch Schultz to integrate his numbers operation in 1932. People's livelihoods were at stake.

But crime also had its consequences. The proportion of deaths by homicide, a figure that included lynchings, was between four and eleven times higher for black people than white in every state of the nation and every major city in 1930 and 1931. Chattanooga had the dubious distinction of being the most dangerous city for African Americans with a 1931 homicide rate of 160.7 per 100,000 population, more than ten times the white rate. These homicide ratios changed little through the decade. Poverty and racism also contributed to the higher conviction and incarceration rate of African Americans. In the first three years of the decade, black men were committed to prisons at three times the rate of white men, black women at four times the rate of white women. Burglary, larceny, and auto theft topped the crimes for black men in these years; homicide, larceny, and auto theft for black women. Interestingly, for these and several other crimes, black convicts received, on average, shorter sentences. Less surprisingly, crimes for which black men received substantially longer sentences included rape and other sex crimes.

Black artists, scholars, and athletes, often supported by New Deal programs, responded to hardship and discrimination in their own ways. Many of them gained the national spotlight, bringing status as well as pride to their communities and demonstrating black ability in every area of public life. At the same time, the often different sensibilities, history, and cultures these individuals brought helped shape or even transform the larger fields in which they worked.

Despite a history of exclusion, African American scientists and inventors made notable contributions in the sciences. Although most white universities continued to exclude black researchers, a few accepted black students for training or hired exceptional black faculty. More gained training and research opportunities in black colleges and universities like Howard, Spelman, Tougaloo, and Tuskegee, often aided by New Deal or foundation funding. A number worked directly for government agencies. Ernest Just explored the regeneration of cells and the process of egg fertilization and chemist Percy Julian synthesized estrogen and testosterone and developed new drugs to treat glaucoma and rheumatoid arthritis. William Cardozo studied sickle cell anemia. George Washington Carver developed a new drug to fight gum disease. Charles Drew pioneered more effective ways to store blood for medical use, particularly ironic given the Red Cross's segregation of blood by race of the donor. Frederick Jones invented an automatic refrigeration system for trucks that allowed for the long-distance shipping of perishables and an air conditioning system for mobile field hospitals. Beyond their specific contributions, this pioneering generation demonstrated that, with training and opportunity, black doctors and scientists could advance human knowledge and the ability to heal.

In a completely different physical realm, athletics, racial barriers were also beginning to fall. Although most major sports like baseball continued to segregate its players by race, several black athletes broke through color bars to succeed in boxing and track and field. Joe Louis became World Light Heavyweight champion in 1935 and World Heavyweight champion in 1937, the first African American to do so since Jack Johnson in 1907. He held the title until 1949. Louis had been defeated by German Max Schmeling in 1936, and given growing anti-Nazi sentiment, both white and black Americans rallied around their countryman for a rematch in 1938. When Louis defeated Schmeling, thousands poured into the streets to celebrate the victory of the "Brown Bomber." For African Americans, the victory was both a moment of racial and patriotic pride and a further challenge to German and American white supremacist ideologies.

Jesse Owens, African American track and field star, had the same opportunity to challenge white supremacy when he competed in the 1936 Olympics in Berlin. Owens broke two Olympic records and won four gold medals. Three other African American athletes also earned gold medals at those Olympic Games. Customarily the German chancellor shook hands with each medalist. In this case, rather than shake a black man's hand and thereby challenge his own claims of Aryan superiority, Hitler left the stadium. Overnight, Owens became an American hero. Ironically, however, the white American coach who ran Owens expressed his own form of bigotry. Owens ran one of his medal-winning races only because the U.S. coach, fearful of upsetting Hitler, barred Jewish teammate Marty Glickman from participating. The Olympics offered a new twist on the now familiar pattern of challenging racism on one front while reinforcing it on another.

But it was in the arts that African Americans made their most substantial cultural contributions. Supported by federal programs, empowered by the greater visibility of black people in all walks of life and the new public rhetoric of equality, moved by the particular hardships that poverty and racism had imposed on black people, a generation of black artists found their voice in the Depression era.

Certainly racism in the arts had always had its own ironies. So many black performers were celebrated by whites who refused to sit beside them or interact socially. This remained the case during the 1930s, as white audiences feted an increasing number of talented black musicians. Many of them, like vocalist Marian Anderson, excelled in traditionally Western musical styles. Caterina Jarboro sang at the Puccini Opera House in Milan, Italy, in 1930, the first African American to sing with a major opera company, and in 1934 the first to perform in an American opera. Margaret Bonds became the first black guest soloist to play with the Chicago Symphony Orchestra. Other orchestras played the music of African American composers William Dawson, William Grant Still, Margaret Bonds, and Florence Price.

But most of these performers, like Billie Holiday, Bessie Smith, Mahalia Jackson, Ella Fitzgerald, and Rosetta Thorpe, came from black musical traditions like jazz, gospel, or blues. What they brought from those traditions changed the course of American popular music by revitalizing its rhythms and deepening its emotional tone. Indeed, it was they who made it popular. In 1936 Benny Goodman, the first white bandleader who used black musicians regularly, hired pianist Teddy Wilson and vibraphonist Lionel Hampton. Edward Kennedy "Duke" Ellington and Fletcher Henderson organized their own bands and performed around the country. Trumpet player Louis Armstrong, fondly known as "Satchmo," and singer Ethel Waters had their own radio shows. Without black musicians there would have been no jazz, no blues, and a far less improvisational and syncopated flair to American popular music.

The emergence of "talkies" in the late 1920s had transformed the movie industry, and many black actors as well as white had celebrated careers. Although Hollywood for the most part continued to stereotype its black characters, Depression-era black film actors like Bill "Bojangles" Robinson, Paul Robeson, Hattie McDaniel, Stepin Fetchit (whose stage name illustrated the extent of Hollywood's racial bias), Fredi Washington, Mantan Moreland, Butterfly McQueen, Eddie Anderson, Clarence Brooks, and Rex Ingram became stars in their own right. Lena Horne made her film debut in 1938, the same year McDaniel became the first African American to win an Oscar as best supporting actress for her role as Mammy in *Gone With the Wind*. Although criticized by some for playing domestic servants, McDaniel frequently responded that she much preferred playing a maid to being one.

But not all films portrayed black people in demeaning ways. Black film-maker Oscar Micheaux produced seventeen films during the Depression, none of which mocked or stereotyped their characters. His *The Exile*, released in 1931, was the first "talkie" made by a black-owned film company. Paul Robeson brought dignity to his roles in *The Emperor Jones* (1933) and *Showboat* (1936). A few hard-hitting movies critiquing racism and its consequences, like *Imitation of Life* (1934), *Showboat* (1936), and *Black Legion* (1937) revealed that serious movies on these subjects could indeed succeed. In *Imitation of Life*, Louise Beavers played a black domestic worker whose light-skinned daughter (Fredi Washington) rejects her in order to pass for white. Hidden black ancestry also motivates the plot of *Showboat*. In that film, Paul Robeson sang "Old Man River," a powerful description of the hardship of life as a black man. *Black Legion* offered an inside view of a racist vigilante group generally understood to be the Ku Klux Klan. Other black actors performed around the country with the Federal Theatre Project. They brought theater to rural black communities and integrated previously all-white stages. A number of FTP plays were written by black playwrights and focused on black experiences, including Rudolph Fisher's "Conjure Man Dies," which opened on Broadway; J. A. Smith and Peter Morrell's "Turpentine"; and Hall Johnson's "Run Little Chillun."

Radio, however, remained mired in racist stereotypes, despite shows by Ethel Waters, Louis Armstrong, and occasional appearances by talented black actors and singers on white shows. The only show about black people, *Amos 'n' Andy*, portrayed the two men as simple-minded ne'er-do-wells seeking their fortune in Chicago. The characters, although clearly African American, were played by white men who exploited genial black stereotypes for the audience's amusement. Like vaudeville, black listeners heard these portrayals in multiple ways. Many, including the *Chicago Defender*, enjoyed the spoofs and found the show lighthearted and harmless. Others insisted it perpetuated racial stereotypes and demeaned all black people. Robert Vann of the *Pittsburgh Courier* launched a petition drive in 1931 to get the show off the air, but the Federal Radio Commission refused to comply. A similar debate arose later in the decade, when Eddie Anderson began to play the servile valet Rochester on *The Jack Benny Show*. Anderson himself insisted he was portraying one hapless character, not an entire race of people, but many saw it differently.

Others made a name for themselves through the visual arts. Most were determined to make their art both beautiful and useful in furthering the cause of black equality in some way. Each piece produced by these men and women challenged white stereotypes about black inferiority. Black artists expanded the repertoire of techniques and sensibilities of American art by bringing their cultural heritage to bear in their work. Asadata Dafora Horton and Katherine Dunham brought African and African American music, rhythms, and patterns of movement into mainstream dance performances. Dunham, considered the progenitor of African American dance, explored dance traditions of Africa and the West Indies in her choreography. She was also the first black choreographer to stage a Metropolitan Opera performance. Painters like Romare Bearden, Archibald Motley, and Jacob Lawrence celebrated the vibrancy and dignity of black life and history, as well as its struggles, in their work. Although each brought a different perspective to his or her work, collectively they embodied both the aspirations and frustrations of the community from which they came.

Many of these artists gained both skills and visibility through New Deal art programs. Lawrence, for example, studied art at the WPA Federal Arts program's Harlem Community Arts Center. Chicago's Southside Community Arts Center and Detroit's Heritage Center offered a venue for WPA artists in those cities. New Deal arts programs also hired Aaron Douglas, Charles Alston, Sargent Johnson, Selma Burke, Richmond Barthe, and Augusta Savage to produce works of public art including large murals and sculptures depicting the power and dignity of American workers to grace government buildings.

Black writers, essayists, and poets were similarly committed to their craft and to their people. Like their colleagues in the fine arts, many found work through New Deal agencies, including Arna Bontemps, Claude McKay, Richard Wright, Zora Neale Hurston, Margaret Walker, and Ralph Ellison. Their literary contributions spanned many genres and topics. Some, like Wright and James Baldwin, critiqued race relations through powerful fiction or political essays like those in Wright's *Uncle Tom's Children* (1938), which won Wright a WPA prize. Wright is perhaps most famous for his 1940 novel, *Native Son*, in which he outlined in dramatic and terrifying detail the impact racism could have on subjected and desperate black people. William Attaway explored the black experience in steel mills in *Blood on the Forge* (1941). Hurston celebrated black southern folklife in novels such as *Jonah's Gourd Vine* (1934) and *Their Eyes Were Watching God* (1937). Others used poetry to express African American responses to racism, poverty, and discrimination, like Sterling Brown's *Southern Road*, Margaret Walker's *For My People*, and Langston Hughes's "Weary Blues" and "Let America be America Again."

The WPA provided both artistic training and an opportunity for children's self-expression through its Federal Arts Program. Here, children in a Jacksonville, Florida, program exhibit their work, based on the theme of "spirituals." 1937. Courtesy of the Franklin D. Roosevelt Library Digital Archives.

Many received broad public recognition for their work. In 1930, for example, Nella Larsen became the first African American to win a Guggenheim creative writing award.

The experience of being black in a racist society shaped each of these writers and many expressed themselves through the political left because they saw its radical potential to change black life. But their views were no more the same than their personalities; there was no single "black perspective." These writers varied in their approach as well as their politics. Scholars have pointed to the more nationalist position of Ralph Ellison, for example, who envisioned black life within a pluralistic American culture that validated and celebrated cultural distinctions. They have contrasted this with the more assimilationist position of writers like Richard Wright, who viewed full integration as the better path to equality.

These writers' focus varied as well, ranging from economic to social inequality and from celebration of black life to lamentation over the consequences of racism. Some placed race at the center of their work. For others, race served as a backdrop for a universal story. Black writers were not uniform in their understanding of what it meant to be "black" or of the proper response to oppression. They were not "representative of blackness" in any crude way, any more than contemporary white writers like John Steinbeck or Ernest Hemingway were quintessentially "white." But as a group, these writers had an important impact on American literature in the way they brought problems of race, racism, and their consequences into public view, and their exploration of the multiple black responses to those issues. Although the center of black literary and artistic life had shifted to Chicago, they continued the work of the earlier Harlem Renaissance writers in demonstrating the humanity and the diversity of black people.

These black musicians, artists, and writers did not simply succeed in American culture, they reshaped it. Each brought different skills and gifts to their art, but they all tapped into a history, a cultural tradition, and a way of thinking that had been shaped by a set of experiences distinct from those of white people. These experiences shaped their styles, their subjects, and their approaches. American music, painting, dance, and literature all bear the mark of black artists. If art shapes a people and their way of seeing the world, then black artists shaped the American people.

Such social ferment had an impact on the scholarly and scientific community regarding beliefs about race. The contributions of African Americans and other minority groups and a generation of work by minority scholars led to the wholesale rejection of racial stereotypes or even the usefulness of race as a physically descriptive category. These new academic approaches to race and race relations did not change appreciably the attitudes of most white people in the Depression decade. They did, however, lay crucial groundwork for the arguments of the future civil rights movement by undercutting traditional arguments about black inferiority.

Both black and white scholars contributed to this new thinking about race and culture. Among African Americans, perhaps none were as well known as W. E. B. Du Bois and E. Franklin Frazier. Du Bois, who had been exploring black history and culture since the turn of the century, published *Black Reconstruction in America* in 1935, which continued his exploration of the impact of discrimination and poverty on black lives. If black lives and opportunities were constrained, then white racism and discrimination, not black inadequacy, had constrained them. Frazier, a sociologist, challenged assertions of the inherent inferiority of black family structure, beginning with the 1932 publication of *The Free Negro Family*. His *The Negro Family in the United States*, which appeared in 1939, emphasized the external pressures affecting black families, although he largely neglected the ways in which the black poor shaped their own lives. Historical experience, rather than any biological or inherited set of abilities or traits, shaped black lives and behaviors, he concluded. Other black historians, political scientists, sociologists and economists, some now less widely known but no less important, made significant contributions of their own to the discussion, including St. Clair Drake, Horace Cayton, Ralph Bunche, Robert Weaver, Abram Harris, John Hope Franklin, Benjamin Quarles, and Charles Johnson.

Several white scholars, many of whom had been publishing on race and culture since well before the Depression, presented similar arguments. Franz Boas, Melville Herskovits, Ruth Benedict, Margaret Mead, Otto Klineberg, Kurt Lewin, and other sociologists, social psychologists, and anthropologists expanded on their earlier works to reinforce the preeminence of culture, rather than biology (or race), in shaping individuals. Characteristics like intelligence, morality, or temperament, they argued, were products of people's upbringing and social experience and were not hardwired into genes. Thus, these scholars explained differences between racial or other human groups on the basis of social structures and patterns and historical experience, not any inherent and unchanging biology.

A few white religious groups also challenged their own racism. In 1931 the Federal Council of Churches prohibited segregation of any church groups using church facilities. Activist Catholics and Jews also began to make common cause with black leaders in Los Angeles, San Francisco, Chicago, New Orleans, Detroit, Baltimore, Atlanta, New York, and a number of other cities to ease frictions between their communities and improve opportunities for all minority groups. These outreach efforts were generally local and limited, but they helped lay the groundwork for later, national interracial coalitions on behalf of universal civil rights.

Important as these efforts were, they also reflected the limits of the liberal vision of race held by so many whites. Optimistically, most of these scholars and activists believed that because black and white people differed only by skin color and not by ability or biology, solving the problem of racism required only raising more open-minded children and attacking general social problems related to poverty and unequal opportunity. White people would come to see black people as just like them. In other words, no specific programs focusing on racial inequality or redress were necessary. But this call to ignore race, and the failure to challenge structural barriers to black opportunity, were doomed to failure because they ultimately reinforced too much of the racist status quo. U.S. society was too rooted in racial distinctions to suddenly begin ignoring them. Its very history rested on the alleged inferiority of black people. Its economy relied in large measure on exploitable black labor, and its civic institutions disproportionately favored whites. Even if individual white people did move beyond their own racism, those structural disparities would remain. This seeming contradiction—that in a racist society one can not erase racism by pretending race does not exist—would continue to challenge civil rights activists in coming decades. For all the successes of black artists, athletes, and scholars in the Depression era, most black people remained mired in poverty and trapped by the forces of both individual and structural racism. Black cultural and communal life could ease the worst of the burden, but it could not overcome it.

Notes

1. Richard Wright, *Twelve Million Black Voices* (New York: Viking Press, 1941, repr., New York: Arno Press, 1969). 130.

2. William Davis, quoted in Doxie Wilkerson, *Special Problems of Negro Education* (Washington, DC: Government Printing Office, 1939), 29.

Epilogue: "Should I Sacrifice to Live 'Half American'?"

As the new decade approached and war loomed ever closer, the American economic landscape began to change. Jobs, particularly industrial jobs, became more plentiful. The government began investing in training programs. Relief rolls declined. Yet, black people's struggles for equal access to opportunity, white resistance, and limited governmental response continued. Meanwhile the heightened intensity of wartime raised the stakes on all sides. This meant more dramatic and visible protests on the part of blacks and sympathetic whites, greater violence from white supremacists, economic improvement, and several real advances for civil rights. Although the war itself is beyond the scope of this book, a glance at these developments as the United States prepared for war reveals how much African Americans had learned from a decade of economic and political struggles.

The New Deal saved Americans from starvation and utter despair, built crucial infrastructure, restructured banking and commercial regulations, trained and educated young people, and solidified Americans' conviction that government had a responsibility to provide for its neediest citizens. What it could not do was end the economic crisis. It took a world war to do that. As the war began in Europe, as U.S. industrial production expanded, and young men disappeared from the workforce to serve in the Armed Forces, the demand for labor exploded. The numbers receiving government relief fell as unemployment plummeted and wages began to rise.

As with the economic expansion of the early twentieth century, African Americans and other minority groups benefited enormously as jobs became more plentiful and wages rose. With expanding labor needs, more employers integrated their workplaces and black employment rates increased dramatically. Nevertheless, racial discrimination persisted in private industry as well as in the military. The number of African Americans on unemployment and relief rolls declined, but not as quickly as for whites.

But the past decade had prepared African Americans to respond effectively. During World War I, black leaders had argued that demonstrating patriotism and quieting civil rights protests until after the crisis ended would result in true equality as grateful whites realized the unfairness of discrimination. That did not happen. The accomodationist strategy had failed. Instead, the Depression decade offered an alternative strategy: community protest that engaged directly with political leaders and programs could bring real change. During the early 1940s African Americans mobilized again, in both private and public venues, to demand equal treatment in all areas of American life. These protests, as well as the unfulfilled promises these protests wrung from white leaders, reveal the legacy as well as the limitations of Depression-era black activism.

The buildup to World War II began in the late 1930s. Each step brought an infusion of money and orders for war matériel to dormant or struggling American industries. Once the United States formally entered the war in December 1941, war production shifted into high gear. Millions of new jobs raised a tremendous demand for labor and dropped the unemployment rate to levels unimaginable even two years earlier. Yet, although the National Defense Advisory Committee urged employers to hire without regard to race or religion, the same discriminatory practices that had constrained African American opportunities during the Depression continued to operate as the nation moved toward war. Many contractors continued to hire only whites for skilled and professional work. They excluded African Americans from training programs and maintained their segregated workplaces. This discrimination extended to the U.S. Employment Service, whose southern branches systematically excluded black men and women from vocational training or jobs in skilled fields. Even the National Defense Training Act, which included a prohibition against racial discrimination, nevertheless favored white applicants. By 1941 fewer than 5,000 of its 175,000 trainees were black. Not surprisingly, then, the number of black workers on WPA rolls continued to grow until the program was terminated in 1943.

The persistence of unequal treatment provoked increasingly public protests from African Americans and their white supporters. The New Deal

Desperate for labor, the federal government not only forbade racial discrimination in war industries, but also promoted racial unity through the release of photographs like these. In this 1942 photo, Philip Leung, Marcell Webb, and an unidentified white worker adjust the landing gear of a plane destined for battle. Courtesy of the Franklin D. Roosevelt Library Digital Archives.

had taught them that government was responsible to all its people and that organized interest groups received benefits. Roosevelt's administration had responded before to claims of racism by inserting antibias clauses in program requirements or by developing special "Negro sections" to monitor hiring patterns. Now, these activists argued, the nation was facing a new kind of emergency and it must respond once again.

These protests extended beyond words. Political coalitions that had formed to expand local job opportunities in the 1930s now broadened their reach to include businesses elsewhere in the city, public utilities, and municipal services. In St. Louis, as in New York, political action won black jobs in the telephone, gas, and electric companies. The NAACP convinced a number of northern hospitals that had refused to hire black doctors and nurses to reverse their policies. The Communist Party, however, which had organized such protests earlier, reversed direction in 1941 after Germany invaded the Soviet Union. Now the party considered its primary mission to defend the USSR. Arguing that race-based protests distracted workers and diverted energy from the cause, Communists called for all such protests to cease until the war was won. For many in the black community, this single decision discredited the party.

Perhaps most dramatic was a protest that did not actually occur. In the spring of 1941 Socialist and labor leader A. Philip Randolph called a meeting of black leaders at the Hotel Theresa in Harlem. His proposal, a massive protest march in Washington, D.C., to demand the integration of the Armed Forces and the prohibition of discrimination in defense industries, caught the imagination of all those present. Although Randolph had long worked in coalition with white allies, he insisted that this venture needed to be made up entirely of black people. This would testify to African Americans' resolve, ability, and power. Desperate to maintain unity during a time of impending war, Roosevelt tried everything he could to persuade Randolph to call off the march. He pointed to the army's officer candidate schools, whose training programs had been integrated the year before. He even sent two of the white leaders most respected among African Americans, Eleanor Roosevelt and New York City mayor Fiorello La Guardia, to talk to movement leaders.

When all pleas failed, President Roosevelt signed Executive Order 8802 in June 1941. The order prohibited discrimination on the basis of race or religion in any union or company receiving a government defense contract, or in any government training program. It also established a Fair Employment Practices Committee (FEPC) to monitor progress. The order fell short of the movement's demands. It did not, for example, compel the integration of the Armed Forces. Given the limitation of the government's power to intervene in private business, the order applied only to those involved directly with defense contracting. Nor did the FEPC have any power to enforce the nondiscrimination requirement even in areas over which it had jurisdiction. In many southern locales, segregationists dominated the War Labor Boards, ensuring that even if racial complaints came before them, they would not be resolved.

As a result, many companies across the South still refused to hire black workers. But the problem extended beyond the South. Black workers filed complaints of discrimination against businesses and unions in many northern cities. In the FEPC's first year of operation, it received more than 6,000 complaints of discrimination, almost 80 percent of which came from African Americans. Fully one-third came from black women. These inadequacies led Randolph to continue his efforts in a March on Washington Movement (MOWM). Its broad goals—desegregation of the military and of public facilities, employment without regard to race, full access to the ballot, and decolonization—would continue to guide activists for decades to come.

Despite its shortcomings, the executive order proved an economic turning point for African Americans. Government had acknowledged its responsibility to remedy employment discrimination where it could, and, given the exploding demand for war production, the order actually affected thousands of companies, especially in shipyards and aircraft production. Both median income and skill level rose within the African American community, and unemployment declined in the years leading up to Pearl Harbor, with even greater improvements to come. The federal government also met its commitment by hiring African American workers directly. Both the number of black federal employees and their job classification levels rose. Some limited change came even within the Armed Forces. In 1941, the air force had opened a training school for black pilots at Tuskegee. Within a year the navy and marines began accepting black men for general service for the first time, although still on a segregated basis.

The economic impact of the rearmament effort was particularly striking for women, both black and white. The proportion of working women exploded in these years, and the opportunities for advancement improved markedly as women became a crucial source of labor. For white women that often meant joining the workforce for the first time. For African American women, who had historically worked in large numbers and had generally been relegated to jobs in domestic service, these years brought new opportunities for more attractive, better paying, and skilled work than ever before. Although white women obtained skilled work more quickly than their black counterparts—and undercut traditional gender divisions by receiving such jobs ahead of black men—the number of black female industrial workers, both skilled and unskilled, rose substantially.

The FEPC also had a positive effect on race relations within the trade union movement. The combination of effective black organizing and government support galvanized black efforts to integrate all-white unions. The FEPC's rules applied to unions that controlled jobs, as well as employers, and wartime demands intensified the need for workers. Although the AFL remained resistant to change, industrial unions made dramatic strides. In 1941, for example, African American workers joined with whites in a strike that led to the unionization of Ford under the United Auto Workers.

The UAW stayed true to its commitment to racial equality. When white workers at Chrysler struck in February 1942 to protest the transfer of black employees into more desirable defense work, the union persuaded management to stand firm, and work continued on an integrated basis thereafter. Elsewhere, however, locals defied the International. Just one month earlier, white workers at Packard's Hudson Ordinance Plant staged a protest after two black janitors were transferred to milling machine jobs. Management returned the two men to their original positions. Despite pressure from national union leaders, the local branch refused to fight for the black workers. It took five months, continued pressure from International, and a strong letter from the secretary of the navy to reunite the men with their milling machines, and sporadic resistance continued for several more months.

That same year CIO president Philip Murray established the Committee to Abolish Racial Discrimination, to educate unions on the benefits of welcoming black workers into their ranks. Other progressive unions like the United Packinghouse Workers and the Marine Cooks and Stewards also continued to press hard for black labor equality. Progress continued to be slow, but aided first by New Deal era labor legislation like the Wagner Act and then by the FEPC, black union members came into their own in the 1940s. In doing so, they transformed not only their own working lives but also the democratic potential of the nation as a whole.

The years leading to war also brought more victories for the NAACP in its continued legal challenges to discrimination. In October 1940, federal district courts ruled that boards of education could not use race as a reason to pay teachers differently. That same year, the Supreme Court issued two important civil rights rulings of its own. The first, *Hansberry v. Lee*, severely limited the reach of restrictive housing covenants. The second case addressed the issue of all-white juries. *Smith v. Texas* overturned the rape conviction of a black man because virtually no African Americans had served on any grand jury there. When black people on trial faced juries that had been deliberately restricted to whites, the court explained, they were denied the constitutional guarantee of a jury of their peers. Each successful decision inspired those concerned with equal rights to persevere on the path laid out by Charles Houston and others in the early years of the Depression. The legal process might be slow but it had already proved a potent weapon in the battle to protect African American rights and expand their opportunities.

Civil rights activists used every opportunity to build on these successes and make their case for full equality. On January 31, 1942, just after the U.S. declaration of war, James Thompson of Wichita, Kansas, wrote a letter to the editor of the *Pittsburgh Courier* asking, "Should I Sacrifice to Live 'Half American'?" The paper responded by announcing a "Double V" campaign tying victory over tyranny abroad with victory over racial oppression at home. As the editors explained, "WE HAVE A STAKE IN THIS FIGHT. . . . WE ARE AMERICANS TOO!"[1]

The campaign caught on. Again and again, in newspaper articles, speeches, and other public forums, African American leaders drew comparisons between the Nazis in Europe and racist whites at home, pointing to the hypocrisy of fighting a war for freedom and democracy while denying them to American citizens. The evident and horrifying repercussions of racism in Europe demanded a rethinking of American racial behaviors and practices. The Double V campaign went further, linking the full participation of black people in the war effort to the Allies' ultimate victory. Denying black opportunity violated both the spirit of the struggle and the likelihood the Allies would win.

Many white public figures also linked racial equality in the United States to victory abroad. In 1941 more than one hundred white labor leaders and Catholic, Protestant, and Jewish clergy signed a statement by the Committee on Negroes in Defense Industries that demanded racial equality to preserve American democracy and to further the war effort. Politicians and scholars, such as Fiorello La Guardia, Pearl Buck, and Wendell Wilkie, added their voices to the growing clamor for racial justice and desegregation. Even the War Department's propaganda arm embraced the sentiment, issuing posters featuring decorated black war heroes, and others of black and white men working together bearing the legend, "United we win."

The linkage between Nazism and racism also galvanized white or majority-white organizations. The Southern Conference for Human Welfare took on so many projects that it divided in 1942: SCHW continued to address political issues while its sister Southern Conference Educational Fund focused on challenges to segregation. The same year, the American Missionary Association created a Race Relations Division. The Union of

American Hebrew Congregations began providing sample sermons for rabbis to deliver on "Race Relations Sabbath."

While anti-Nazi rhetoric spurred this liberal political action, the intellectual underpinnings about the dangers of racism came largely from continued academic research. If racism turned Germans into Nazis, its malignant power had to be fought directly. Using the new social scientific understandings about prejudice developed by black and white scholars in the 1930s, the American Council on Education and American Youth Commission collaborated on studies of the impact of racism on personality. Two of the most important volumes in that series, John Dollard's and Allison Davis's *Children of Bondage: The Personality Development of Negro Youth in the Urban South* (1940) and Charles Johnson's *Growing Up in the Black Belt: Negro Youth in the Rural South* (1941) painstakingly uncovered the real costs of racism in the loss of human potential. In the same years the American Jewish Committee began funding social psychological studies of racism and anti-Semitism, an effort that would continue for over a decade.

Many of these works considered racism primarily from the individual point of view, this time of the racist. They emphasized racism as a psychological state, a mental illness that was equally dangerous for the individual and for the nation as a whole. Social scientists argued that prejudice and racism were the products of the individual racist's frustrations, and not attitudes inherent to all human beings. Nor did the behaviors of those whom the racist despised produce them. Racism was a fiction that hurt both the bigot, whose real frustrations were not addressed, as well as the targets, who were unfairly stereotyped and penalized. Such views gained governmental support in the report of the 1941 White House Conference on Children in a Democracy, which concluded that children did not inherit prejudice but learned it. They could therefore unlearn it if Americans made a collective effort to challenge both prejudice and discrimination wherever it appeared.

Placing responsibility for racism on white people was a tremendous step forward from so many earlier studies that claimed black physical and intellectual inferiority. But this focus on the individual largely failed to recognize the structural elements of racism, arguing, in essence, that the way to change the racism of American society was to change people's attitudes by teaching tolerance and open-mindedness. The rest would then largely take care of itself. To its credit, the White House conference also emphasized the importance of dismantling institutional racism, calling on governments, trade unions, schools, social agencies, and others to do their part to equalize services and opportunities. Inequality, they insisted, was inimical to democracy. Policymakers and academics joined political leaders in their calls for change.

Perhaps the most public expression of the contradiction between fighting racism abroad while supporting it in the United States came from Swedish sociologist Gunnar Myrdal, who was hired by the Carnegie Foundation to detail the economic, social, and political realities of African American life. In the final report of this research, his two-volume *American Dilemma* (1944), Myrdal concluded that racial discrimination so deeply violated the American creed of equal opportunity that the nation could not bear the contradiction forever. Ultimately, he argued, white Americans would have to resolve this dilemma by either fulfilling the American promise for all or repudiating it entirely.

Too few white Americans agreed with such antiracist arguments. Instead, the huge migration of African Americans to industrial centers and their improved economic standing, both the result of wartime economic expansion, increased racial tensions and intensified white resistance to black equality. Like earlier population surges, this new black migration increased overcrowding, heightened demands on housing stock, and worsened job competition. African Americans' anger and frustration grew alongside their sense of promise, as the high expectations created by new employment opportunities and wartime's rhetoric of equality clashed with the realities of continued hardship and struggle.

Meanwhile, many working-class whites, themselves struggling and frustrated, resisted the influx of these threatening newcomers. Racist stereotypes overlaid by economic competition produced sometimes violent results. Residents of white neighborhoods attacked any black families trying to move in and destroyed their belongings. In 1941 whites in Detroit called for the new Sojourner Truth federal housing project, designated for African Americans, to be a white project instead. As the first black families prepared to move in at the end of February the following year, hundreds of agitated white protesters ringed the housing complex and a fight ensued. Fortunately no one was killed, but forty were hurt. The police made 220 arrests—217 of them African American. Protests continued until the National Guard finally mobilized at the end of April to protect the black families. Unfortunately, this episode proved to be only a prelude to the even larger and more violent riot that was to come the following year.

The military mobilization, which brought northern black men to southern army bases, also produced both heightened black expectations and racial friction. These northern recruits ran afoul of segregation practices they did not understand or refused to accept, and their resistance empowered some southerners to do the same. Just in 1941 and 1942, Birmingham police reported more than fifty cases of black men and women refusing to follow segregation laws. In Memphis, the arrest of a black woman for refusing to move to the "black" section of a bus prompted more than 2,000 African Americans to demand change from the mayor.

Such acts of resistance, which expanded on Depression-era tactics, continued to gain traction. The interracial Congress of Racial Equality (CORE), formed in 1942, led the way. Borrowing a technique from the industrial union movement, its leader Bayard Rustin used what he called "sit-ins" in hotels and restaurants that refused to serve black customers. If denied a room in a hotel, for example, Rustin spent the night on a chair in the hotel lobby. This tactic, of course, exploded across the South in 1960 after a group of college students sat at a Woolworth's counter in Greensboro, North Carolina, but it had been pioneered long before.

White residents felt deeply threatened by such challenges to segregation because they demonstrated that these black men and women were not appropriately deferential to whites or white privilege. As protests grew more common across the South, violations of the southern racial code brought harsher words, beatings, and arrests. One such case in Mobile in 1942 resulted in the shooting death of a black soldier by a white bus driver. The resulting black protest compelled the bus company to disarm drivers and to promise to enforce segregation laws fairly. They did not desegregate the buses, nor were they asked to by local protest leaders. The southern black political restraint of the Depression era continued to operate well beyond the Depression itself.

If deference meant enduring humiliation, however, local whites were correct. Black soldiers were not deferential to whites. Many fought back, whether the attacks came on the base or off. Indeed, within two years of the U.S. entry into the war, a number of these confrontations exploded into full-scale race riots, suggestive of the deep anger and fear lying beneath the surface. Most of these riots were launched by whites, and black people and other minority group members under attack fought back. The Depression era had helped propel African American demands for equality that would be resisted, but would not be stopped.

Despite all the advances of the early 1940s, it would take another two decades for laws against employment discrimination to reach across the country or for the gap between black and white earnings to close further. Nor was there much evidence that the greater open-mindedness of some white leaders on the race question had filtered down into the broader white community. The gap between official and clerical pronouncements of racial equality and the reality of continued discrimination had lessened a bit since the start of the Depression, but it had not closed.

Nevertheless, once African Americans demonstrated that they could perform well at any job, their abilities could never again be easily denied, nor the antidiscrimination protections dismantled. African American electoral power had grown with the expanding northern black population. This new political clout, along with the greater willingness of black citizens around the country to engage in political action of various kinds, made any government retreat on civil rights commitments impossible. While few were as optimistic as Gunnar Myrdal, whose *American Dilemma* proclaimed the inevitability of a "redefinition of the Negro's status in America," none could deny that a sea change had begun.[2]

In the reshaping of the economy, the new understanding of governmental responsibility to its citizens, and the struggle against fascism, the New Deal era set the stage for the civil rights revolution that was to come. The successes of political organizing, the mutual support of community action, the expansion of economic and educational opportunities, and a renewed sense of possibility helped shape the black community that would undertake that revolution.

Notes

1. "The Courier's Double 'V' for a Double Victory Campaign Gets Country-Wide Support," *Pittsburgh Courier*, February 14, 1942. The campaign had been introduced without fanfare the week before. Thompson's letter had appeared in the January 31 issue.

2. Gunnar Myrdal, *An American Dilemma: The Negro Problem and Modern Democracy* (New York: Harper, 1944), 997.

~

Documents

Employment and Unemployment in the Depression

The government normally takes a census of its inhabitants every ten years. The 1930 census therefore provides information on (among other things) the employment situation at the start of the Great Depression. The economic collapse prompted another census in 1937, focusing on unemployment. Notice the racial and gender differences in employment at the start of the Depression, the different impact the Depression had on each type of employment, and the impact of race and gender on who lost their jobs. At the start of the Depression, African Americans were already clustered in low-level jobs such as service and unskilled factory labor. Black men had worse jobs than white men, generally speaking, and black women had worse jobs than white women. The lower the level of skill, the more likely workers of both races were to be unemployed or underemployed, but in virtually every category and for both sexes, once again African Americans fared significantly worse than did whites.

Black and Native-Born White Gainful Workers in the U.S. by Race, Gender, and Socioeconomic Status, 1930, by Percent

	Native White		Black	
	Male	Female	Male	Female
Total	100%	100%	100%	100%
Professional	4.5	16.8	1.5	3.3
Proprietors incl. farm, managers, officials	25.5	4.6	23.0	4.7
Clerical	15.5	37.1	1.7	1.1
Skilled	16.8	0.8	4.8	0.1
Semiskilled	14.1	24.8	9.0	10.1
Unskilled:				
Farm	9.7	2.7	18.9	22.8
Servant	1.3	11.8	9.4	56.3
Factory and other	12.6	1.3	31.7	1.7

Unemployed, Partly Unemployed, and Emergency Workers, 1937 per 1,000 Gainful Workers in that Occupational Group (1930) by Sex, Race, and Occupational Group

Race, Occupational Group	Totally Unemployed		Partly Unemployed		Emergency Workers	
	Male	Female	Male	Female	Male	Female
White	108	155	69	50	44	33
Professional	51	38	23	14	34	19
Farmers, tenants	21	11	21	5	9	1
Proprietors, managers	20	17	9	5	7	5
Clerical	76	119	28	32	25	26
Skilled	105	74	88	43	48	49
Semiskilled	161	167	122	95	48	37
Farm laborers	150	149	114	52	60	12
Other laborers	147	78	95	31	73	11
Servant	123	130	53	49	34	16
Negro	144	186	99	71	59	26
Professional	101	191	58	50	67	73
Farmers, tenants	24	16	33	17	4	1
Proprietors, managers	48	32	36	15	18	8
Clerical	130	449	63	95	63	160
Skilled	221	—	159	—	117	—
Semiskilled	232	322	158	101	89	75
Farm laborers	145	53	155	33	28	3
Other laborers	155	164	91	57	78	26
Servant	171	168	81	80	55	14

Source: U.S. Department of Commerce, Bureau of the Census, *A Social-Economic Grouping of the Gainful Workers of the United States*, Washington, DC, 1938, p. 10; U.S. Department of Commerce, Bureau of the Census, *Final Report on Total and Partial Unemployment 1937*, Vol. 1, Washington, DC, 1938, p. 6.

～

A Leader Feels the Strain

Mary McLeod Bethune, activist and organizer, was one of the greatest black lead-ers of the twentieth century. In 1904 she founded the Training School for Negro Girls in Daytona, Florida, which by 1931 had developed into the coeducational Bethune-Cookman College. She remained its president until 1942. Bethune also served on the boards of many civic, black, and women's organizations, helped found the National Association of Colored Women's Clubs in 1896, and the more politically oriented National Council of Negro Women in 1935. She served as spe-cial adviser to President Roosevelt for minority affairs and Director director of the Division of Negro Affairs of the National Youth Administration. She and First Lady Eleanor Roosevelt were friends.

Nevertheless, Bethune faced moments of self-doubt. She found her work daunt-ing, and the task immense. In the black community, the uneducated needed to be taught and the educated needed to step up to their responsibility to help. Racial change was needed locally and nationally but white leaders would not act without pressure. The institutions that developed to deal with these issues—several of which she founded or led—lacked adequate funding. Bethune made all these her goals. But even someone as capable and optimistic as Bethune had moments where she felt overwhelmed. In the letter below, Bethune writes to George Arthur, an African American "Associate for Negro Welfare" of the Julius Rosenwald Fund, estab-lished to improve black education. Bethune discusses the financial difficulties facing her as president of Bethune-Cookman College. The letter is a plea for funds, as Bethune found it impossible to balance her other political obligations with the need to raise money for the college. But it is also the cry of a woman at the end of her emotional rope, worn out from the struggle.

Mary McLeod Bethune Pleads for Help, 1930

Nov. 1, 1930

My dear Mr. Arthur,

May I tell you again how grateful we are for your visit to Bethune-Cook-man and for the opportunity you gave me to so fully converse with you, and the encouragement, light and information that came to me from this con-tact. I am thanking God for you and your interest and want to ask that you, possibly in a childlike way, adopt me as your big sister, and help to direct and guide me, and possibly take the unusual interest in the thing that I am trying so earnestly to do in Florida.

I do feel the need for some earthly stay; somebody to have pride in my efforts. I do feel, in my dreamings and yearnings, so undiscovered by those who are able to help me. I have been pulling along so long, fighting an unusual battle in an exceptionally difficult section of our country. But during these years, something has happened. A great change has come about and if at this critical moment, we can get the right shove-off, it will possibly save me for many more years of general service to humanity.

The burden is so heavy just now, the task is so great, that speedy reinforcement is needed. My mind is over-taxed. Brave and courageous as I am, I feel that creeping on of that inevitable thing, a break-down, if I cannot get some immediate relief. I need somebody to come and get me. The struggle has been long and courageous. I need help, not to tax me more, but help that will give me immediate relief. It is possible that my Maker permitted me to come into existence to serve in my way at just such a time as this. I feel I still have a larger contribution to make to the general masses. They are clamoring for the same inspirational counsel that I am permitted to give here, there and everywhere. Shall I be spared for this or shall I fall under the strain of this heavy burden-bearing? I think the time has come for my friends and philanthropic organizations to answer yes or no.

I spent two very interesting days of service in the White House conference last week. It seems necessary that I be one of the inter-racial group that will tour the southern schools early this month. . . . Organizations and groups are clamoring for me all over the country. With these opportunities for unique service and for making the contribution that the Negro womanhood of America needs to make today, if I am to fit into such a program, money worries for carrying on should be lifted from me. I believe there is relief. Will you help me find it? . . .

Do you know any source from which I could get a fund for publicity purposes and the unfolding of the work I am doing. . . . My own life's story should be gotten together and sent out. I think this is the psychological time for it. I feel so helpless within myself without funds to get these things over. Will you think about it and tell me what you think of it?

I would like to have you consider the traveling scholarship for some of the heads of our departments, so that we might . . . be able to make contacts with different educational organizations and investigate schools so as to keep abreast with the best methods. . . .

Please give me any definite instruction you may have on just what your organization may be in position to assist us in doing. I shall breathlessly await a reply from your board in answer to my application. Some immediate relief in the general running is my strongest plea just now. . . .

I have written you rather fully. I hope you understand my heart-pulse on the whole subject. No egotism is aimed at, at all, but I wanted to talk understandingly with you. I want you to feel free to write me and to suggest to me and to help me in any way you can.

Source: Mary McLeod Bethune to George R. Arthur, Nov. 1, 1930, Box 174, Rosenwald Fund papers, Fisk University, Nashville, TN.

〜

Southern Farm Families Tell Their Stories

In 1939 a group of writers and scholars in the Works Progress Administration set out to document how people responded to the Great Depression. Sensitive to poverty and hardship, they paid particular attention to the experience of poor and minority workers and families, those least likely to appear in the history books. Here Tom Doyle, father of a southern farm tenant family, and Grace Turner, mother of a sharecropping family, share their lives with Federal Writers' Project interviewers, and with us.

Notice the variety of living arrangements, the deplorable housing conditions, a farming family's daily schedule, the ways families struggled to make ends meet, the nature of credit purchasing, and how families built meaningful and fulfilling lives despite such hardships. Notice too that New Deal programs barely touched their lives. The difficulties these families experienced were common to many southern black farm families during the Great Depression.

Notice too how unproductive and irrational the southern farming system was for all involved. Landowners did not allow their tenants or sharecroppers to plant for self-sufficiency or to improve the soil because these would have enabled their farm hands to escape debt. Denied decent schooling and the vote, tenants had little recourse against cheating. The costs to tenants and sharecroppers are obvious. Better hidden but no less real were the costs to landowners and to the region as a whole. Crop diversity would have raised prices and therefore profits for planters. Better education and soil conservation would have increased productivity in numerous ways, raising everyone's standard of living. Racism and class exploitation kept the South poorer than any other region of the country.

"I Has a Garden": A Farm Tenant Family

"Them's my boys," Tom said proudly. Already it seems that the five-room house can hold no more. By count it shelters twelve, from the eighty-year-old uncle of the second wife to the latest arrival of last year.

The boys came into the yard, two tall healthy fellows about twenty years old. They stopped by Tom's chair and told him of the day's work. They had been helping a neighbor harvest his peanuts and each will receive a dollar when the crop is sold. . . .

There was a little chill in the air. Tom turned to the uncle, "Hit's gettin' cold, old man. You'd bettah go on in." The old man, his thin knees punching bags into worn bottle-legged trousers, . . . tottered to his feet with the aid of the wife and went indoors. . . .

"He's the third old pusson I'se taken care of," Tom said, referring to the uncle. "Fust there was my stepmammy. Then when I ma'ied that woman"—nodding at the woman on the porch—"she brung her uncle to live wid us. The one before that was ninety year old. His name was Toby Neal. No, he wasn't no kin to me. Just said he'd rather stay wid me than anybody he knowed. I tole him I was a pore man but if he wanted to live wid me I'd be glad to have him."

"Tom's got a good heart," the second wife interrupted in a low voice.

"I was bo'n in '89. I'm what they calls a off-child—my mother wasn't ma'ied to my father. . . .

"My mother didn't have no education and my father just had a common one. He went up to the third grade in school and got to be a deacon. My gran'daddy was a tenant and he didn't have no education neither. Hit was funny 'bout him, he couldn't read his name if hit was writ a foot high 'gainst the side of the house but he could figger as good as the next man. One day . . . he dug out a big bunch of peanuts and carried them up to the house. That night he set down befo' the fire and counted off a hundred. He taught me to count wid them peanuts. . . . He made me go thru the fourth grade too. My . . . gran'mammy was as good to me as she could be. She didn't have much of a education neither and her father was a tenant. . . .

"When I was nineteen I . . . went to work for Coy Blake, a colored feller what owned a little farm. I worked for wages and stayed wid him a year. He give me eleven dollars and fifty cents a month and boa'd and then threw in a acre-and-a-half of peanuts so's I'd have somethin' toards the end of the year.

"Mr. Bill Bunting, a white gentlemun, went halves wid me on some of his land. He give me eleven acre of good land and paid me fifty cent a day to help him when I wasn't workin' on my crop. He give me a fifty dollar order on a town store. Mr. Yates who run the store charged ten percent in trade; he let me trade forty-five dollars wuth wid him and I paid him fifty dollars at the end of the year. His goods costs high. When we sold the corn 'n peanuts 'n cotton off that piece and I paid my half of the fertilizer and pickin', I cleared a hundred and twenty-seven dollars. It was the fust time I ever had a hundred dollars. I like to a-shouted.

"Me'n my wife felt pretty good. I had got ma'ied to a gal nineteen year old and she was pretty smart. We had a little two-room house that was right comf'table.

"That next year Mr. Bunting give me thirteen acre and a dollar a day widout boa'd when I was workin' for him runnin' the peanut bagger, fifty cent a day when I was plowin'. My wife worked wid him too when he had need of her. That was beside goin' halves wid him on the thirteen acre and it come in mighty handy 'cause I made from a dollar and a half to three dollars a week sometime for workin' wid him.

"Somethin' else I did. I took that twenty-seven dollars and paid out'n it for my share of the fertilizer, and I didn't run no account at the store. It sure opened my eyes when I seen how much cheaper you could buy things for cash. That yeah I cleared two hundred dollars. In them two years we had one chile, a boy chile, and we had the midwoman. Midwomen only charged five dollars and the doctor would'a charged twenty-five dollars.

"The next year I quit Mr. Bill Bunting and went back wid Coy Blake. I 'greed wid him to rent nineteen acre of ornery land for fifty dollars and then I went down to Mr. John Bales and paid fifty dollars for a blind mule. Everthing went along all right until my wife come down wid another chile.

"The midwife got the chile out all right. It was another boy. But my wife was young and strong and she wanted to he'p me so she went out too soon and worked in the field. She took sick. I had the doctor and did everthing I could but she died with buth cold. She weren't but twenty-two year old. I didn't think nobody that young could die. Hit was a funny feelin' 'thout nobody to cook 'n wash 'n look atter the chillun. Hit was kinda lonesomelike.

"The doctor bill took more'n I had and when I give him all the money I had left out'n that two hundred dollars . . . I still owed him eighteen dollar and a half. I told Coy Blake he could take the crop and the mule if he'd square me wid the doctor and bury my wife. He give me forty dollars to bury my wife wid but he wouldn't square me wid the doctor like he say he would. He got the crop and the mule.

"I went to Belhaven and got work with a big saw mill. They paid me a dollar and a half a day. I wouldn't stay at the camp. Nossuh, I got me a room in a colored hotel. It took most of what I made to live wid and send money back to my wife's father. He was keepin' my chillun for me.

"I stayed at the sawmill for six month then I come back and got ma'ied to that woman yonder. I rented twenty-five acre from Mr. Glass and moved out wid my two chillun and that woman's two chillun. She had two gals. That year I got off sixty-four dollars. You see, I got started so late I didn't have no time to raise food for my mule and my wife and the chillun. I had to run a account wid the store. My wife did have a mule that she got from her firs' husband and that cut down on hit a little. Nossuh, you know I didn't ma'y that woman for her mule! Well, Mr. Glass charge me a hundred dollars for rent and the store charge me three hundred dollars for what I got so I come out bad sixty-four dollars. That woman had a boy. We used a midwoman. . . .

"I started out wid seventeen acre but now I rents sixty-five acre of land . . . and lets my [married] boy have part of the crop and use one of my mules. I got four mules. They's twelve here in this house and down my son's place they is five. I pays Mr. Dunne four hundred and eighty-five dollars rent. I spends two hundred and fifty dollars for fertilizer and the store run me 'bout three hundred and fifty dollars a year.

"The store is for my son's family and mine too; 'bout a hundred and fifty dollars of hit is for clothes and the rest for food and things about you need. I has a garden wid collards 'n' cabbage 'n' tomatters 'n' I raises my own meat. . . ."

Tom led the way down to the pen and proudly displayed eight large hogs. "They're Berkshire and Poland China," he explained. . . . In a field in the woods he had other hogs. Asked if he used the county agent much, he replied that he heard from him about once a week. Sometimes he does what the agent suggests, then sometimes he doesn't, depending on how the advice looks to him.

On the way back through the neat barn, Tom . . . detoured by way of the hen house. "The hogs is mine and these here chickens is that woman's." In the house were about a hundred fat hens, barred rocks and other straight breeds. "She makes about three dollars a week offen the eggs of these here chickens," Tom said. Other sheds house tools, a V-8 and model A Ford. The latter belongs to his oldest son.

Back at the house, Tom opened the door of the living room. A lamp had been lit and a fire made in the silver-painted tin stove. Faded paper covered with tiny pink roses covered the walls. On one side of the stovepipe was a colored picture of Joe Louis sparring with a white man. Tom went to New York to visit "that woman's" oldest daughter last summer and brought back the picture as a memento of a place he wouldn't live in. There was a carpet on the floor and a two-piece living room set, upholstered chair and sofa. Several assorted chairs were in the room. There was a battery radio and a winder phonograph. On the side table were a few china figures of the kind given away as pitchpenny prizes at the fair. . . .

Life in the country is the only life for Tom. It isn't like life in town, all cluttered up. He can get his wood and his water free on the farm. He wouldn't live in town.

He doesn't think the owners he's worked for have done as well by him as they might have. The houses they have given him weren't as good as they could have provided. The sitting room is the best room in this house. He had to paper it himself. The other rooms, some of them, leak pretty bad and he has to repair them. His chief grievance is that they haven't given him sheds to put his tools and machinery under or his cars; he has had to build them. He owns a hay baler and rents other machines. He also thinks they charge him too much rent for the land.

"What does I want? I got a option on a farm now. I'm hopin' the government's gonna help me get it. The county man's already been out and 'proved it. Guess I've paid eight thousand dollars rent these last seventeen year and I don' own a foot of land. I want 'bout a hundred acre of cleared land, 'nough for me and all these chillun of mine to work on. I want it good land and I want a good lil' house on it. . . .

Source: Willis Harrison, Edwin Massengill, "I has a garden." From THESE ARE OUR LIVES by the Federal Writers' Project, Regional Staff. Copyright © 1939 by the University of North Carolina Press, renewed 1967. Used by permission of the publisher.

"Tore Up and a-Movin": A Sharecropping Family

"We hain't had no Christmas here, not a apple or a nut or nothin': I told the chil'en not to look for no Santa Claus this year, but to thank their God if they had meat and bread." Gracie Turner . . . leaves her wash tub in the back yard to show the way to the cheerless fire-place where green wood smolders.

"Dis here is my father, Sam Horton. He has seen some years. He's ninety-one and in tole'ble good health, except his 'memb'ance ain't strong and he can't eat much grease. I've been takin' care o' him now for seven years, best I could. For the past three months he's been gettin' seven dollars and a half for de old age pension, and dat's been a help here.

"Dat's Ola in de corner." Gracie indicates an attractive mulatto girl who looks almost dainty in spite of her ragged clothes. Her feet are bare. "Ola is twenty-four. Awhile back she married a drinkin' man, but he scrapped so bad she couldn't stay wid him; so she come back home to live. Dis girl is Amy, fourteen years old. She's got bad kidney trouble; her leg swells up big as two sometimes. Dr. Simpson started givin' her treatments in de clinic, but she ain't had none in some weeks now." Amy is also barefooted.

"De littlest boy is Raymond Farmer. Dr. Farmer 'fore he died named him for his brother, Judge Raymond Farmer. Stephen is de oldest boy at home. Sam and Will belongs to my daughters, but I raised 'em. . . . Wid my husband,

James Turner, and Papa and me, dat makes nine of us to stay in dese two rooms. . . .

"Most of us sleeps on dese three beds in here where we keeps de fire. In here is de kitchen. Mr. Jake Anderson give me dat range; it's de one Miss Bettie fust cooked on when she was married." The old stove is coated with grease, but the kitchen is orderly. . . .

"Right across de hall is de other bedroom. . . . De girls covered dese chairs and dis settee wid de flowered cloth deyselves. Dat victrola ain't no good now. We tries to keep dis room sort o' dressed up for comp'ny, but dey ain't no fire in de heater; so we better set in de fireplace room. Today's a cold day if you ain't about stirrin'.

"Now, 'bout de other chil'en: Hattie May lives on some island down here 'bout Portsmith —Hattie May Williams she is now. Her husband does public work and seems to be a right good man, but I didn't know where he'd be good to Hattie May's Will or not. May married Montgomery, and dey sharecraps for Miss Sallie Simpson over toward Benton. Edward's married and farms for Mr. Peter Ellis at Martinsburg. Lillian Turner—now I can't tell you 'bout her, 'cause I hadn't heard from her in three years. Marcy works for rich folks in Philadelphia. She sent us a box o' old clothes 'fore Christmas, and dat's de onliest string we've had this fall. De rich folks is always givin' Marcy wrist watches and necklaces and things for presents. Dey sends her down town any time wid a hund'ed dollars to buy things for 'em, and she takes every cent back to 'em it don't cost. Dey has learnt to trust Marcy. I's tried to raise my chil'en to be trusty and mannerable, to mind dey mama and papa, to be honest. 'Show favor to your mother and father,' I tells 'em, 'dat your days may be lengthened on God's earth.' If dey does wrong it shore ain't 'cause I hadn't tried to learn 'em right.

"Dey ain't been much schoolin' for none of 'em. Will's in de fif', and Lillian got to de ninth. None de rest got past de fou'th grade. Turner went to school enough to write his name, but he can't do no figgerin' to 'mount to nothin'. I never went a day in my life, can't write my name or add or keep track of our account on de farm. I want dese youngest chil'en to go long enough to do dat much.

"'Tain't no while to say dis is de hardest year we's ever had. Every year's been hard, de forty-nine years I been here. Dat's all dey is to expect—work hard and go hongry part time—long as we lives on de other man's land. Dey ain't nothin' in sharecrappin', not de way it's run. My folks has always share-crapped. . . . When I married Turner, we lived in Hawley, Virginia, 'bout six months. He done public work, railroadin' and sech dere. From Hawley we moved to a farm near Gum Springs, where we worked by de day for a year.

From dere we moved to my brother's and sharecrapped for him five years. Den we moved to Mr. Calep Jones', where we stayed three years. Next we moved to Mr. Hughes Whitehead's and farmed wid him two years. Our next move was to No'th Ca'lina on Mr. Jake Anderson's farm at de Woollen place. We stayed wid him thirteen years. Den last year we moved here to de Willis place, dat Mr. Dick Henry rents from Mr. Bob Willis in Gum Springs, and here we is now. But we got to move somewhere dis next year. Another man's a-comin' here. I don't know where we'll go; houses is sca'ce and hard to find. Mr. Makepeace told Turner he'd help him all he could, but he ain't got no house we can live in. Plenty o' land everywhere, but no house! Turner has been huntin' a place for weeks, and every night when he comes home I runs to de door to hear de news. Every day it's de same tale: 'I hadn't found no place yet.' I hates to move; nobody knows how I hates to move!

"We left Mr. Jake Anderson 'cause he didn't treat us right. Me and him fussed de whole thirteen years we stayed dere, and I said if I kept livin' wid Mr. Anderson I'd go to de devil shore. . . . We always had trouble settlin' wid Mr. Anderson. One year I got me a book and ask him to set down everything he charged us wid in my book, so I'd have it in his own figgers when de year ended. But he said he wouldn't have it dat way; one set o' books was all he aimed to keep. So den I got to askin' him every week what he was chargin' us wid, and my daughter set it down. At de end o' de year we got Mr. James to add it up on de addin' machine. We handed it to Mr. Anderson when we went to settle, and it made him mad. He said we'd settle by his figgers or get off'n de place, dat nobody should keep books but him on his farm.

"Another time when we wanted a car, he bought us one over in Weldon, but made us put up the two mules we owned den against de car. De boys was in a wreck and damaged de car right smart. Mr. Anderson come and took in de mules and de car too. After he had it fixed up, we tried to get him to sell it back to us. He wouldn't, but went and sold it to another man. So we was lackin' a car and mules too.

"We never made nothin' much wid Mr. Anderson. De most we cleared was $179, after we'd paid out, two years. Most years it was fifty and sixty dollars after de account was paid. Every settlement day me and him had a round. I'd tell him he had too much charged against us, and he'd say I was de fussin'est woman he ever saw, and to go to de devil! De last year we was wid him we made 'leben bales o' cotton and three hund'ed bags o' peas. When we settled, we didn't have accordin' to his figgers but five dollars for our part o' de crap, nothin' to buy a string o' clothes wid, nothin' to eat but meat and bread. We left him. We had to sell de hogs we raised to eat to buy us some clothes. We hadn't never got no rent money. I said somethin' to Mr. Anderson last time

I saw him 'bout de rent. We needs it for clothes and shoes; the chil'en's feet is on de ground. It made him mad; he said he hadn't got no rent. Turner went over to Benton and ask about it. Dey said it wa'n't right, but Mr. Anderson was holdin' de cotton and peas for higher prices dey reckoned; de rent would come by 'n' by dey reckoned. . . .

"Mr. Henry come home 'fore Christmas and 'pears to be all right now. We hadn't had no settlement wid him yet, but he told us dey wouldn't be nothin' for us this year, not to look for it. De account on de book 'gainst us is $300. How it got dat much I can't tell you. We raised 224 bags o' peas and 1800 pounds o' seed cotton on twenty acres. I knowed we couldn't make no crap, wid just twenty-four bags o' plaster 'lowed us to fertilize twenty acres. We was just about to get hongry here, with all de money cut off and no crap comin' in. Long as dey was cotton to pick or peas to shake some of us could get a day o' work now and then, enough to buy a sack o' flour and a little strip o' meat. Work has been sca'ce dis fall though. So Turner got him a WP and A job a-diggin' stumps. He's done had three pay days, $12.80 at de time, though he don't get but $12 'cause eighty cents has to go to Mr. Sickle for haulin' him to work. I makes dat twelve dollars do all it will, but dey's eight of us to live out 'n it four weeks to de month.

"Turner ought not to be a-workin' wid de WP and A. De gover'ment's got no business a-payin' out relief money and a-givin' WP and A jobs to farmers. De old age pensions is all right for old folks dat's 'flicted and can't do. Take Papa dere; he can't work in de field now. He knocks up our wood to burn in de fireplace, but he's seen too many years to get out and work by de day. But able-bodied landers has got no business a-havin' to look to de gover'ment for a livin'. Dey ought to live of'n de land. . . .

"I always tries to raise my meat and bread and lard, collards and sweet 'taters for de winter, and a gyarden for de summer. I keeps a cow. Milk and butter and biscuit is de biggest we live on now. . . . I believes de bugs dats eatin' up stuff now is sent 'cause folks is so mean. If dey don't do better, plagues is goin' to take de land. I tries to live a Christian, tell de truth, and be honest, but de world is full of dem dat don't. It ain't often I gets to church. I hadn't been in over twelve months. . . . I hadn't had nothin' fittin' to wear to church lately; de chil'en neither. . . .

"Farmin's all I ever done, all I can do, all I want to do. And I can't make a livin' at it."

"I reckon I soon farm as anything else," Amy observes.

"I rather go in service. I want to be a cook or a maid for white folks," Ola adds. "I can cook some already and I could learn more."

Gracie raises her head, but she remains downcast in spirit. "Dis year has been so hard we've had to drop our burial insurance. We enrolled wid de burial association in Ga'ysburg some years back. All it costs is twenty-five cents when a member dies. But day don't come many twenty-five centses in dis house.

"Every night I prays to de Lord: 'Please keep death off till I get out'n dis shape.' Dey ain't a decent rag to bury me if I was to die right now, and I hates for de county to have to put me away."

Source: Bernice Kelly Harris, "Tore Up and a-Movin.'" From THESE ARE OUR LIVES by the Federal Writers' Project, Regional Staff. Copyright © 1939 by the University of North Carolina Press, renewed 1967. Used by permission of the publisher.

〜

Black Women at Work

Long before the Depression, the Department of Labor's Women's Bureau had been studying the experiences of women in the workplace. African American and immigrant women worked far more often than white women, particularly among those who were married. Thus, the Women's Bureau paid a good deal of attention to race.

The Depression posed particular hardships for working women. As the Bureau pointed out, the Depression affected every worker, but men and women experienced it differently. Race also continued to play a role in shaping the work experience, because so many employment opportunities depended on whether the worker was black or white. Thus black women bore a double burden, facing discrimination for both their race and their gender. The following is an excerpt from a 1938 Women's Bureau pamphlet that surveyed black female workers in various regions and fields, documenting their specific experiences and particular struggles. The report concluded with the social and economic costs of discrimination, and a reminder that any improvement in black women's employment conditions would require programs and regulations that addressed their distinct needs.

The Negro Woman Worker

One of every six women workers in America is a Negro, according to the latest [1930] census figures. . . . How many of these women now have jobs and how many are unemployed; where the employed women are working; how much they earn, and how their wages compare with those of white women workers: these are questions that have a direct bearing on the economic problems of today.

Though women in general have been discriminated against and exploited through limitation of their opportunities for employment, through long hours, low wages, and harmful working conditions, such hardships have fallen upon Negro women with double harshness. As the members of a new and inexperienced group arrive at the doors of industry, the jobs that open up to them ordinarily are those vacated by other workers who move on to more highly paid occupations. Negro women have formed such a new and inexperienced group in wage employment. To their lot, therefore, have fallen the more menial jobs, the lower paid, the more hazardous—in general, the least agreeable and desirable. And one of the tragedies of the depression was the realization that the unsteady foothold Negro women had attained in even these jobs was lost when great numbers of unemployed workers from other fields clamored for employment. . . .

On the whole, most women, white or Negro, work for their living just as do men, not because they want to but because they must. The reason larger proportions of Negro than of white women work lies largely in the low scale of earnings of Negro men. . . . Practically 2 in 5 Negro women, in contrast to 1 in 5 white women, work for their living. . . .

In 1930 about 9 in every 10 Negro women still were engaged in farm work or in domestic and personal service, with more than two-thirds of them in domestic and personal service. . . .

In 1930, 3 in 5 Negro women workers reported their usual occupation was in domestic and personal service. Included in this . . . were . . . domestic employees in private homes; . . . laundry and cleaning . . . ; housekeepers and stewards, . . . waitresses; . . . untrained nurses and midwives; . . . hairdressers and manicurists; . . . charwomen . . . ; and elevator tenders. . . .

Today, 8 years after that census, it is certain that the plight of Negro domestics since the beginning of the depression has been an exceedingly serious one. . . .

From common knowledge, and according to the few recent scattered studies that are available, low wages and long hours are characteristic of household service. . . . Inadequate living and working conditions on the job were reported for many households. In a number of homes no bathing facilities were provided for the workers; too often the bed was found to consist of a cot in the living room or furnace room. Long hours and heavy work were characteristic of many jobs and the difficulty of managing children constituted another problem. . . .

Many Negro women have found work in one or another of the branches of public housekeeping, as cooks, waitresses, chambermaids, cafeteria counter girls, and so forth. . . . Though hours tend to be shorter and better standardized in public than in private housekeeping, the workweek of the woman in a hotel or restaurant is likely to be much longer than that of the woman in factory, store or laundry. . . .

A relatively new occupation for Negro women workers is that of beauty service. . . .

Most of the Negro women were serving the needs of their own race, but a few were at work in white beauty shops or barber shops. . . .

[Their] earnings reported to Women's Bureau . . . were low. The average weekly wage was . . . about three-fifths that of the white women in the industry. . . . Hours were very long. . . .

Long as may be the hours of the Negro domestic worker, low as may be her earnings, . . . in general the economic status of these workers is much more favorable than that of the Negro woman agricultural laborer. For this woman worker there are few aspects of her working life over which she has any real control. Crop conditions, markets, and prices; the employment status of her family, whether as owners, tenant farmers, sharecroppers, or wage workers; the necessity of accepting field work as one of a family group . . . ; lack of educational facilities, particularly in the rural South, which would enable her to equip herself for other employment if it were available—these are some of the factors that materially affect her living. . . .

A marked trend from tenant farmer to the lower status of sharecropper is shown for Negro labor in the South . . .—a trend not shared to the same extent by the white agricultural group. . . . A brief but vivid description of the Southern sharecropper-system was given by a Negro woman sharecropper at a . . . conference sponsored by the Joint Committee on National Recovery: . . .

> Since they stopped using fertilizer the clothes are very scanty, because we could take fertilizer sacks and make aprons and dresses for the little children. But since they are not using fertilizer very much you just can't hide their nakedness thorough the winter. . . . And some of them haven't even got houses to stay in as good as lots of common barns. And some families of 12 and 14 live in houses with maybe one room and kitchen, with maybe three beds where 10 or 12 are sleeping, . . . and not even have a flue for the stove pipe to go in, and the stove is setting out in the floor. And . . . when you start a fire you will get smoke all over the house until it gets started burning good, and you have to stay outside until it starts burning good because it smokes you out. Families have to put up with all kinds of things like that. . . .

[A] survey of agricultural labor conditions in Concordia Parish, La., issued by the United States Department of Agriculture in October 1937 . . . concludes [that it] . . . : "presents a picture of the evolution of the old plantation with its slave labor emerging as a unit operated with cropper or wage labor. The position of its laboring class has not changed materially from that of earlier times." . . .

Disheartening as are the present circumstances of Negro agricultural workers in the South, the future seems to hold even more serious threats to their economic security. . . .

Tenancy in the Old South is the successor to the slave system. Both institutions were, in different ways, devices for holding on the land, on a subsistence basis, sufficient labor to meet the maximum seasonal requirements of agriculture. As a result, the Southeast is now drenched with labor and is therefore especially vulnerable to all forces which may cause the displacement of workers. The depression, followed by the crop-reduction program, has already forced some displacement of tenants. Much greater displacements may be caused in the near future as a result of technical developments. . . .

Negro women in what may be termed "white collar occupations"—in transportation and communication, trade, public service, professional service, and clerical occupations—totaled only about 5 percent of the Negro women gainfully employed [in 1930]. On the other hand, native white women in the same occupations totaled . . . 56 percent of all gainfully occupied white women of native birth. . . .

Naturally there are many reasons for this disparity in the proportions of Negro and white workers in the better paid, more highly skilled, occupational fields. Educational facilities for Negro workers are notoriously inadequate in some sections of the United States. Negroes have had a relatively short span of years in which to demonstrate their ability in certain fields requiring training and skill. But there is an additional reason of much significance, which is clearly suggested in a recent publication of the Works Progress Administration of Georgia. . . :

> The shift downward [in the employment status of formerly white-collar Negro workers] . . . was caused by the depression. White-collar occupations among Negroes depend, for the most part, upon the Negroes themselves. The doctors in the main have only Negro patients; . . . and Negro teachers must teach in Negro schools. Negro business has a limited market, as it is confined to the Negro group. During a period of retrenchment, certain phases of white-collar work continue while others disappear. . . . Generally there is nothing else but to go to lower occupational levels.

With the great bulk of Negro workers, men and women, receiving wages that permit of only the barest subsistence . . . the reasons for the limitations of Negro white-collar opportunities become plain. . . . Increased white-collar employment among Negro workers inevitably will follow a rise in the economic status of all Negro wage earners. . . .

The public must pay heavily for the substandard working and living conditions of many thousands of Negro women workers. When people have no jobs or their wages are too low for adequate support, they still must have food, shelter and clothing. The presence on relief rolls in 1935 . . . of one in every four Negro women workers, and the fact that two-fifths of these unemployed women were the economic heads of families, constitute a situation that is of grave import to the citizens who must support these women and their families.

Experience has shown further that low living standards are costly in that they breed crime and disease, which affect all citizens. Workers desperate for jobs are the prey of unscrupulous employers, who by using cheap labor are able to undercut employers willing to pay fair wages. . . . Such workers are available as strikebreakers. When a significant proportion of the population is forced to live at a substandard economic level, all classes . . . are deprived of the benefits resulting from adequate purchasing power in the hands of those who would spend if they could.

Because of the relation of the problems of Negro women to those of other community groups, it might be helpful to discuss certain measures for improving the economic status of Negro women that seem most practicable and realistic at the present time. . . .

In general, woman labor has benefitted markedly from social and labor legislation during recent years. . . .

Unfortunately, Negro women workers have by no means shared equally with white women in the benefits of these provisions. Workers in agriculture and domestic service . . . have been exempted from the coverage of most of the laws. . . .

Take minimum wage laws . . . rough estimates . . . indicate that only about 1 in 10 of all Negro women workers are covered. . . .

Schools are badly needed also for vocational training. . . .

But it is far simpler to talk about the economic problems of Negro women workers and to suggest possible remedies than it is to take definite action toward their solution. These problems have taken deep root in the social and economic structure during past decades, and only untiring effort on the part of Negroes themselves, aided by the Nation's socially minded citizens, will succeed in eradicating them.

Source: Jean Collier, U.S. Dept. of Labor, Women's Bureau, *The Negro Woman Worker* (Washington, DC: U.S. Government Printing Office, 1938).

⁓

The State of African American Education

African American schools, segregated by law in the South and by practice and residential patterns in most northern cities, suffered by comparison with those of their white counterparts. They generally received less funding, met in substandard buildings, and had higher pupil-teacher ratios, fewer courses, and poorer supplies. As a result black children received poorer educations and therefore faced worse prospects for the future. African American education had long posed a challenge to reform-minded thinkers, black and white, who lamented not only the unfairness of inadequate public education for black children, but also the wasted opportunities of undeveloped minds. In this article from Survey Graphic, *Gould Beech, an Alabama journalist and progressive reformer, explains the conditions of black schools, the historical and structural reasons for their inferiority and contemporary efforts to improve them.*

Notice Beech's calls for federal aid to education and the teaching of African American history to both black and white students, and his insistence on the relevance of class as well as race in school performance. All these, rarely discussed in Beech's own time, became central issues in later discussions of educational inequality.

Schools for a Minority

Booker T. Washington . . . once observed that it was "too great a compliment to attribute to the Negro child the ability to gain equal education for one dollar to every seven spent on the education of the white child." Thirty years have not altered the fact which inspired the observation. And yet even against such handicaps, the Negro race has advanced in little more than three generations from 80 percent illiterate to better than 80 percent literate—a heartening measure of capacity to make bricks with such straw as there is.

In the plantation area of the South or in the teeming slum districts of Harlem, the Negro boy or girl finds that color determines in varying degree the quantity and quality of educational opportunity. It may be a 15–to–1 difference in the outlay per child enrolled, as in some Mississippi Delta and South Carolina Tidewater counties; or it may involve only comparisons in the age and attractiveness of school buildings and the relative ability of teachers, as in New York or Chicago. It may be that the Negro child attends mixed schools in California, Illinois or Connecticut, and is the victim of individual discrimination on the part of teachers or fellow pupils. But in the case of all but a negligible portion of this one tenth of our population, there is a *difference*.

Educational discrimination is only one phase of the Negro's . . . status, but it is perhaps the most vital standard by which his participation in American life is measured.

Outside of the eighteen states and the District of Columbia where segregation is mandatory by law, the Negro's role in education varies considerably. In most northern metropolitan centers, there is a *de facto* segregation based upon residence. . . .

The factual background, which must take into account the relative poverty of the region may be summed up in general terms:

The Southeast has 12 percent of the nation's wealth with which to educate 25 percent of the nation's children.

These eleven states rank uniformly at the bottom of the list in every significant quantitative index of education. . . .

For each dollar spent on the education of the average child in the nation, the South spends 50 cents for each of its white children, 14 cents for each of its Negro children. . . .

In expenditures for buildings, school equipment, transportation, vocational education and libraries, discrimination is even more marked. . . .

Public graduate and professional training comparable to opportunities for white students in public universities and colleges has been non-existent.

In addition to these discriminations in formal education, the adult southern Negro finds himself barred from such advantages as lecture courses, concerts, theaters, and not infrequently from public libraries and museums.

Within the Southeast there is a wide variation in Negro schools, ranging from a few city high schools which approximate the facilities for whites, to the "schools" in the plantation area. In this area the country school for Negroes is frequently not a school building at all but a church, the lodge hall of a burial society, or an abandoned tenant shack, sometimes without heat, windows, or the most primitive sanitation. In such schools pupils, ranging in age from six to eighteen or older, sit on rude benches or discarded church pews. They lack blackboards, writing materials and adequate books. Some states . . . provide textbooks for Negro schools. Though these are apt to be hand-me-downs, they are far better than no books. But in hundreds of rural Negro schools there is absolutely no teaching material except a few old readers. . . . Due to differences in background and in educational opportunity, including irregular attendance because of poor health, undernourishment, insufficient clothing, and the demands of farm work, almost half of all Negro pupils in the South are enrolled in the first and second grades.

But even with meager equipment and short school terms, a surprisingly large number of teachers succeed in imparting the rudiments of schooling to their pupils. . . .

By no means all of the school plants are substandard. There are several thousand rural Negro communities with attractive and adequate buildings. In the movement to provide such facilities, the Julius Rosenwald Fund has played an important role. Through gifts totaling $5 million, this foundation stimulated the construction of schoolhouses and homes for teachers valued at six times that amount, most of them for Negroes. . . .

Philanthropy has played an important part in other aspects of . . . Negro education. . . . [However] it is expected that within a few years the resources of the major foundations active in supporting Negro education will be exhausted. Already there has been a sharp decline in aid from these sources. . . .

Without minimizing either the extent or the seriousness of racial discrimination, it should be recognized that race is not the sole factor in school inequalities. Most Negroes are in the low income strata; to a large extent they live in rural areas, though this is changing. . . . Wherever the Negro's present status is based upon economic discrimination or rural-urban differentials, the problem ceases to be one of race. It affects white tenants and unskilled laborers as well as Negroes. . . .

It has been an open practice to divert funds allocated by the state for Negro schools to the support of white schools—the whites do the voting, they are the ones to be pleased. . . .

Attention has been focused upon dollars and cents differentials, but there is a growing consciousness of a type of discrimination which cannot be measured in such terms. It has to do with the content of education, both Negro and white. From the first grade, whether he is reading stories of fairy princesses, Biblical characters, or George Washington, the Negro child comes in contact only with white heroes and heroines. The curriculum, which has been identical with that of the white schools until recently, has not given him the emotional security which familiarity with the contributions of his race to American history would afford. For example, he has not known (nor have his white neighbors) that Negroes fought and died for freedom at Bunker Hill and on many other Revolutionary battlefields.

[However] there has been a heartening change for the better. During the last six years . . . the study of race relations is now recognized as an essential responsibility of education.

For two decades the Southern Commission on Interracial Cooperation has been paving the way for this change through . . . the sponsorship of interracial institutes for teachers and the publication of its research materials. . . .

What course, if any, is likely to gain for the Negro a greater relative opportunity in the educational system? . . . Progress will include changes on a thousand fronts—many of them seemingly minor . . . and involving concessions on the part of local school boards, changes in the personnel of state administrations, and the actions of Negroes in their . . . communities. . . .

Second only to the hardships imposed upon the Negro is the hardship laid upon the whole South by its failure to prepare this third of its population to make a maximum contribution to the development of the region. Given the opportunity, the Negro would be able to assume a far greater share of the responsibility of providing social services for himself and for others. The new emphasis upon health services, old age pensions, aid to dependent children and mothers, and the like, will exact an increasing toll, a toll which should be distributed over as great an area as possible. In addition, the Negro could and would contribute more adequately to such bi-racial necessities as law enforcement and highways.

Even ignoring questions of humanitarianism and simple justice, economic considerations are compelling. Negroes remain the custodians of almost half the South's farm land and more than half of its children. Soil erosion and hookworm refuse to recognize the color line, as do certain of their by-products—inefficiency, ignorance, and dependency. And as the welfare of the South is dependent upon opportunity for the Negro, so indirectly is the welfare of the nation.

The mouthings of sectional demagogues, South or North, should not be allowed to obscure the necessity of federal subsidies for education. If there is to be any far-reaching improvement in educational opportunity for the present generation in the rural South, black and white, such help will be essential. As long as the working population of the South remains backward, the region will continue to be a doubtful asset (or even a liability) economically, and at times politically.

There will not be any immediate or widespread demand for a federal program designed to aid rural education, since those who would be most benefited, Negro and white, are inarticulate and politically impotent. Is not the failure of these groups to be . . . aggressive in their own interests evidence enough of the precarious position they . . . occupy in the democratic processes?

Source: Gould Beech, "Schools for a Minority," *Survey Graphic* 28, no. 10 (October 1939): 615–18, 640–41.

~

To Ask for an Equal Chance

Although the New Deal promised aid to all who needed it, racist local administrators and traditional patterns of discrimination limited dramatically the level of support African Americans received. The imbalance was particularly pronounced in the South, although it operated everywhere. Few African Americans had any recourse if their local program administrator rejected their request for aid. They knew no one with power to overrule these decisions, and if they complained they risked provoking local whites into violent retaliation.

Thousands, however, tried a different approach, and wrote to New Deal agency heads in Washington, D.C., or to President Roosevelt or his wife. For the first time since Reconstruction, the federal government was paying attention to poor people and to black people. And so, for the first time, African Americans believed they had a friend in government. While few of the thousands of letters addressed to the Roosevelts or New Deal administrators received personal answers, the descriptions they contained offer a vivid and intimate window into the lives of these neediest of Americans and the blatant racism they encountered. They also reveal the letter writers' pride and willingness to work; no one was seeking handouts. Rather, these writers considered themselves hardworking and worthy citizens who deserved help. What follows is a tiny sampling of letters sent by black women during the Depression years. Notice the difference between the individual pleas of the southern letter writers and the more political appeal of the writer from the North. The late dates of the last two letters remind us that not all the Depression's hardship eased with the coming of war.

Millen, Ga.
February 4, 1935
U.S. Department of Agriculture
Extension Service

Dear Friends:

I am a widow woman with seven head of children, and I live on my place with a plenty of help. All are good workers and I wants to farm. I has no mule, no wagon, no feed, no grocery, and these women and men that is controlling the Civil Work for the Government won't help me.

. . . I wants to ask you all to please help me make a crop this year and let me hear from you. . . . Yours for business.

Mosel Brinson

P.S. These poor white people that lives around me wants the colored people to work for them for nothing and if you won't do that they goes down to the relief office and tell the women, "don't help the colored people, we will give them plenty of work to do but they won't work.". . . Now I am living on my own land and I am got a plenty of children to make a farm, and all I wants is a chance, and I am not in debt. I wants a mule and feed, and gear and plows, and a little groceries and guano. Please help a poor widow woman one year. Please help me to get a start, I will try to keep it.

New Orleans, La.
April 18, 1941
Mrs. F. D. Roosevelt

Dear Mrs.

I am a Negro girl of 25 yrs. I'm sick. I been sick 4 months. I'm in need of food and closes. I don't have any relative at all so help me. I hop I'm not asking so much of you but I hop you would help me, Mrs. Roosevelt. I'm righting you this morning I dont have food for the day. I gose to the hospital. The dr say all my sickes is from not haveing food.

I was working on the NYA . . . 10 month. They laid me off because I was sick and diden give me nothing to live off after tune me off. . . . I'm rooming with a old lade she dont have a husban. She give me food when she have it but she dont have it all the time. I own her 5 month rent right now. . . . If I dont be able to pay her in 2 week she going to put me out. I dont have nobody to go to for help and no where to go what I going to do if she put me out.

Could you do something for me help me to fine something. Tell me what to do if you could give me some to do . . . any where I will do it. I will take a day job are a night job anything. Please help me. You can see I'm in need of help Mrs. Roosevelt. Will you please help me I can live much longer without food. Have lot of micine to take I do take it but it wont do me any good without food and if the lady put me out I just no I will die. . . . Please wright at once as soon as you can. . . .

Thank you. Your kindes will never be forgoting.
Yours sincerely.
Mabel Gilvert
Please do some thing for me at once any thing. Pleasanywhere pleas.

Woodland Park Bitely, Mich.
April 23, 1941
President Roosevelt

Dear Sir:

We are the colored women Democrat club. We are sending in a plea for help for our people of our community. Our men are out of work and have ben for sometimes.

We can't get any Welfare help unless we sign our homes over to the welfare. We do not want to be beggers. Our men would work if they could only get work to do. We have helped in every way we could to help make your third election a success. We have some hard things to undergo during the time we were campaigning but the victory was well worth the pain. . . .

We here in this community are having a tuff way to go just now. There were a lay off just after Jan. and our men were laid off. Any time anything happens like this our group are always the first ones to get the first blow. We have tried to get work. We are sending our plea to you feeling sure you will and can help us in our needy condition. We aren't getting a fair deal. Some of our boys are being drafted for service for our country and here we are in a free land are not aloud to work and make a living for their wives and childrens. You are the Father of this country and a Father are suppose to look out for all of his children so we are depending on you.

From the Colored Womens Democrat Club. We are hoping to hear from you soon.

Yours truly
Lutensia Dillard

Source: WPA Papers, Boxes 119–2 (Brinson to USDA Extension Service); 119–6 (Gilvert to Mrs. Roosevelt; Dillard to President Roosevelt), Moorland-Spingarn Research Center, Howard University, Washington, D.C.

⁓

Shootout near Reeltown

In 1931 Alabama sharecroppers, tenant farmers, and farm laborers of both races founded the Sharecroppers' Union with the help of the Communist Party. Not surprisingly, local white landowners and government officials met their every action with intimidation and violence, culminating in the 1931 shooting death of Ralph Gray, one of the union's founders. In response to Gray's killing, members armed themselves for self-defense. In December 1932, creditors of African American farmer Clifford James demanded that the sheriff seize his livestock in repayment of his debts. Black union members confronted the authorities at James's farm and shots were exchanged. Three union members, James, John McMullen, and Milo Bentley, were killed. Several others were wounded. Five union members, including Ned Cobb, were convicted of assault with a deadly weapon and served jail time.

Such vigilante violence was all too common in this era when workers stood up to employers and when black men and women stood up to whites. John Beecher, an Alabama poet and activist, immortalized the event in his poem, "In Egypt Land." The story is repeated, although with slightly different details, by Ned Cobb in his autobiography All God's Dangers.

"In Egypt Land"
"You"
Cliff James said
"nor the High Sheriff
nor all his deputies
is gonna git them mules."
The head deputy put the writ of attachment back in his inside pocket. . . .
"I'm going to get the High Sheriff and help"
he said
"and come back and kill you all in a pile."

Cliff James and Ned Cobb watched the deputy whirl the car around
And speed down the rough mud road. . . .
"He'll be back in an hour," Cliff James said
"If'n he don't wreck hisself."
"Where you fixin' to go?" Ned Cobb asked him.
"I's fixin' to stay right where I is."
"I'll go git the others then."
"No need of ever-body gittin' kilt," Cliff James said.
"Better gittin' kilt quick
than perishin' slow like we been a'doin'" and Ned Cobb was gone . . .
and though Cliff couldn't see him
he could see him in his mind
calling out John McMullen and telling him about it
then cutting off east to Milo Bentley's
crossing the creek on the foot-log to Judson Simpson's . . .
Cliff couldn't see him
Going to Mr Sam or Mr Bill about it

No
This was something you couldn't expect white folks to get in on
Even white folks in your Union.

There came John McMullen out of the woods
Toting that old musket of his.
He said it went back to Civil War days
And it looked it
But John could really knock a squirrel off a limb
Or get a running rabbit with it. . . .
Cliff James watched his family going across the field . . .
And soon they would be in the woods. . . .
They would just have to get along
Best way they could
Because a man had to do
What he had to do
And if he kept thinking about the folks belonging to him
He couldn't do it
And then he wouldn't be any good to them
Or himself either.
There they went into the woods
The folks belonging to him gone
Gone for good
And they not knowing it
But he knowing it. . . .

When the head deputy got back
With three more deputies for help
But not the High Sheriff
There were forty men in Cliff James' cabin
All armed.
The head deputy and the others got out of the car
And started up the slope toward the cabin.
    Behind the dark windows
The men they didn't know were there
Sighted their guns.
Then the deputies stopped.
"You Cliff James!" the head deputy shouted
"come on out. . . .
we got something we want to talk over."
Maybe they really did have something to talk over

Cliff James thought
Maybe all those men inside
Wouldn't have to die for him or he for them . . .
"I's goin's out" he said.
"No you ain't" Ned Cobb said.
"Yes I is" Cliff James said
and leaning his shotgun against the wall
he opened the door just a wide enough crack
for himself to get through
but Ned Cobb crowded in behind him
and came out too
without his gun
and shut the door.
Together they walked toward the Laws.
When they were halfway Cliff James stopped
And Ned stopped with him
And Cliff called out to the laws
"I's ready to listen white folks."

"This is what we got to say nigger!"
and the head deputy whipped out his pistol.
The first shot got Ned
And the next two got Cliff in the back
As he was dragging Ned to the cabin.
When they were in the shooting started from inside
Everybody crowding up to the windows
With their old shotguns and muskets. . . .
Of a sudden John McMullen
Broke out of the door
Meaning to make a run for his house
And tell his and Cliff James' folks
To get a long way away
But a bullet got him in the head
And he fell on his face
Among the dead cotton plants
And his life's blood soaked into the old red land.

The room was full of powder smoke and men groaning
That had not caught pistol bullets
But not Cliff James.
He lay in the corner quiet

Feeling the blood run down his backs and legs
But when somebody shouted
"The Laws is runnin' away!"
he got to his feet and went to the door and opened it.
Sure enough three of the Laws
Were helping the fourth one into the car. . . .
There by the door-post was John McMullen's old musket
Where he'd left it when he ran out and got killed.
Cliff picked it up and saw it was still loaded.
He raised it and steadied it against the door-post
Aiming at where the head deputy would be sitting
To drive the car.
Cliff only wished
He could shoot that thing like John McMullen. . . .

Source: John Beecher, "In Egypt Land," in *One More River to Cross: The Selected Poetry of John Beecher*, ed. Steven Ford Brown (Montgomery, AL: NewSouth Books, 2003). Used with permission of the publisher.

⁓

Call for a National Negro Congress

In 1935, concerned that the New Deal was not benefitting black people as well as it might, more than 300 black leaders gathered at Howard University to discuss "The Position of the Negro in the Present Economic Crisis." Many expressed the desire to create a coordinating body to advance black interests and civil rights. John Davis, lawyer and leftist, took up the challenge, inviting all organizations concerned with black people to come together to form a coalition that would coordinate their individual efforts. In this widely distributed pamphlet, Davis laid out the arguments for forming such a coalition, describing the problems facing black farmers, industrial workers, women, and young people. Only by motivating African Americans and whites to challenge the existing racist and exploitive economic system, Davis argued, could the situation be fundamentally changed. To coordinate the efforts of liberal and leftist organizations he proposed a new National Negro Congress to provide a framework for such coordination.

Let Us Build a National Negro Congress
In this deepening crisis of monopoly capitalism, of which the existing industrial depression, with its myriad and varied concomitant social disabilities

and degradations, is an acute manifestation, the Negro in politics, industry, education and his entire social life, is faced with a decisive and imperative challenge, to develop and fashion a new and powerful instrumentality with which, not only to arouse and fire the broad masses to action in their own defense, but to attack the forces of reaction that seek to throttle Black America with increasing Jim-Crowism, segregation and discrimination. It therefore seems eminently proper, timely, fitting and necessary, that a National Negro Congress, which will express the struggle of the Negro on all fronts, such as civil and political liberties, labor, social service, politics, fraternal and church interests, through the respective organizations, be held. . . .

[From all] Negro homes must arise the determination to act together to end poverty, to struggle for freedom from the curse of color, and national degradation. Only the unity of action of the widest masses determined to strike out boldly against intolerance and injustice to Negroes can solve the problems facing us today. . . .

To be a Negro is to be robbed of the protection of law. Daily, black citizens are slugged and beaten by thugs wearing the badges of officers of the law. Then they are dragged into the courts whose "justice" is a mockery to democracy. White juries, from which Negroes are systematically excluded, cry "guilty" with utmost ease. . . . What does it matter that the whole world knows the Scottsboro boys to be innocent? Alabama "justice" needs their burnt black skins as a token of white supremacy and to keep the Negro in his "place." . . . Meanwhile thousands of Scottsboro boys in Alabama and the rest of the South die, convicted by lily-white juries. What does it matter that Georgia wants to send Angelo Herndon to 20 years of living death on a Georgia chain gang simply because he led a delegation of hungry citizens to demand bread for their hungry mouths? Of what importance is it that daily newspapers announce the lynching of Claude Neal as they would a circus? . . .

To be a Negro is to be the victim of lynching and lynch terror especially designed to prevent Negroes from seeking any improvement in their social and economic position. The riddled bodies of lynched Negro sharecroppers in Alabama are the answers of plantation owners to their attempt to get an increase from 30 cents to $1 a day for cotton picking. . . . Meanwhile these symbols of death instil [sic] fear in the minds of tens of thousands and serve effectively to subjugate a whole race. Yet a federal government refuses to even enact a federal law to prevent the atrocity of lynching. . . .

"Lily-white primaries" from which Negroes are excluded, by special permission of the United States Supreme Court, determine who shall be the rulers of the South and the nation, while black citizens are voteless. . . . Negroes are barred from public [facilities]. . . . The Negroes are barred from participation in benefits derived from Federal and state funds created by taxation on Negro and white alike. . . .

For Negroes there is no such thing as civil rights. . . . Written laws are forgotten, but the unwritten law that being black is a badge of inferiority is strictly enforced.

Race hatred is distilled at a rapid pace in the public press. Residential segregation and its attendant evils are on the increase. In the North and West even the few civil liberties that were once the proud boast of a few Negroes are dwindling away. . . . What Hitler Germany is today for Jews this country promises soon to be for Negroes in every part of the nation, even greater than now. . . . The very heart of democracy—free speech, the right freely to assemble, and the free press—are being made meaningless. . . . We will be back to the days of Dred Scott, when the Negro had no rights a white man was bound to respect. . . .

Why is it that today Negro citizens in America are . . . resentful of fascist Italy's attempt to plunder Ethiopia? Negroes in America feel a deep sympathy for . . . oppressed Negroes elsewhere in the world. . . . Ethiopia's call . . . for help in her struggle against the mad fascist dictator and to maintain her national independence reaches the heart of every Negro American, and rightly so.

But . . . Negroes [also] know . . . Italian aggression in Ethiopia . . . means a world conflict of nations. . . . As Negroes and as workers they have a stake in peace. War means hundreds of thousands of Negro youth going to rot and die in a fight against other young men rotting and dying, with neither group knowing what under the sun they are doing shooting at each other. . . .

What can be done in the face of these grave problems? At no time in history and in no place have Negroes failed to struggle. Today is no different from the past. The traditions of Nat Turner and Denmark Vesey, of Frederick Douglass, Harriet Tubman and Sojourner Truth are symbols of a militant spirit among Negroes which does not die.

On every hand there are evidences of this spirit. We see semblances of this tradition in the struggles of the National Association for the Advancement of Colored People to win for Negro children equal school facilities, to win for the Negro in the South freedom from mob-violence and lynching; in the fight of the National Urban League and the International Brotherhood of Sleeping Car Porters to organize Negro workers into unions which fight for decent wages. It is alive today in thousands of Negro churches where voices are lifted to defense of Ethiopia and human rights. That spirit lives in the militant fight spirit of Angelo Herndon and in the efforts of hundreds of thousands of Negro citizens to win his freedom and that of the Scottsboro boys. It is apparent in a thousand ways where Negro citizens have banded themselves together to fight against economic and social oppression.

Today larger and larger numbers of men, women and youth of other races fight with them for their freedom. The white sharecroppers of Arkansas, no less than white intellectuals and workers in the North, are in the fight for justice for the Negro.

But hopeful as these signs are, Negro Americans must face clearly the spectre of poverty and oppression and be ready to act now. . . . There is not one of the problems presented in this pamphlet which does not call for immediate action. . . .

It is a realization of this fact which has led a well-known group of American citizens from every section of the country to join together in a call for a *National Negro Congress* and to issue this pamphlet as a means of presenting to American citizens everywhere the need for such a Congress. . . . The Congress is called to meet in the city of Chicago, Illinois, February 14, 1936, on the historic occasion of the anniversary of Frederick Douglass. . . .

The *National Negro Congress* will be no new organization. It will not usurp the work of any organization. It seeks to accomplish unity of action of already existing organizations on issues which are the property and concern of every Negro in the nation.

It is with these objectives clearly in mind that we propose for discussion and action of the Congress the points outlined below:

1. For the right of the Negroes to jobs at decent living wages and against discrimination in trade unions and elsewhere . . . for the organization of Negro workers with their white fellow workers into democratically-controlled trade unions.
2. For relief and social security for every needy Negro family, and for genuine social and unemployment insurance.
3. For aid to the Negro farm population, to ease the burden of debts and taxation, for the right of poor farmers, tenants and sharecroppers to organize and bargain collectively.
4. For the fight against mob-violence, lynching and police brutality; for the right to vote, serve on juries and enjoy complete civil liberties.
5. For complete equality for Negro women; for the right of Negro youth to equal opportunity.
6. To oppose war and fascism, the attempted subjugation of Negro people in Ethiopia, the oppression of colonial nations throughout the world; for the independence of Ethiopia. . . .

Source: John P. Davis, National Negro Congress, *Let Us Build a National Negro Congress* (Washington, DC: National Sponsoring Committee, National Negro Congress, October 1935). Permission courtesy of John P. Davis Papers.

～

Advancing the Race and Its Women

Nannie Helen Burroughs, writer, activist, and president of the National Training School for Girls in Washington, D.C., spoke at a forum held at Bethel AME Church on December 20, 1933. Burroughs began her talk by criticizing accommodating or self-serving black leaders who did not fight hard enough for black advancement, labeling them "Uncle Toms." It was in the Depression decade that black people began to speak disparagingly rather than admiringly of Uncle Tom, the hero of Harriet Beecher Stowe's famous nineteenth-century novel, Uncle Tom's Cabin. *Formerly viewed as a symbol of Christian piety and humility, whose suffering ignited such sympathy from northern whites as to imbue the Civil War with its moral force, Tom now seemed to the newly politicized and activist black community like a spineless lapdog.*

Burroughs called for greater black pride and assertiveness. Unity rather than competition for individual advancement would move the black community forward, she argued. Partway through the speech, Burroughs shifted her attention to black men, whom she accused of being lazy and self-aggrandizing, living off the hard work and generosity of black women. Black women, suffering from both race and gender oppression, often perceived themselves at the very bottom of the heap.

Burroughs gives voice to all this in her brief but powerful call to action. The militancy of her words, and her insistence that black people must not wait for leaders but must rise as a community, call to mind the passionate rhetoric of the later grassroots civil rights and feminist movements, reminding us once again of the importance of the Depression era in shaping those titanic struggles for justice.

Unload your "Uncle Toms"

Chloroform your "Uncle Toms." The Negro must unload the leeches and parasitic leaders who are absolutely eating the life out of the struggling, desiring mass of people.

Negroes like that went out of style seventy years ago. They are relics. . . . I don't care whether they are in the church as the preacher, in the school as the teacher, in the ward as politicians—the quickest way to get rid of them is the best way, and the sooner the better. . . .

They have sold us for a mess of pottage. We get the mess, but not the pottage. The question, "What am I going to get out of it?" must get out of our thinking. This race would have been one hundred years advanced if it had not been for this thought uppermost in the minds of our so-called leaders. . . .

Don't wait for deliverers. . . . I like that [biblical] quotation, "Moses, my servant, is dead. Therefore, arise and go over Jordan." There are no deliverers. They're all dead. We must arise and go over Jordan. We can take the promised land.

The Negro must serve notice on the world that he is ready to die for justice. To struggle and battle and overcome and absolutely defeat every force designed against us is the only way. . . . Men must have life, the opportunity to learn, to labor, to love. . . . We must not give up the struggle until this is obtained. . . .

There must be no compromise.

The Negro is oppressed not because he is a Negro—but because he'll take it. Negroes . . . Stop apologizing for not being white. . . .

Organize yourself inside. Teach your children the internals and eternals, rather than the externals. Be more concerned with "putting in" than "getting on." We have been too bothered about the externals—clothes, money. What we need are mental and spiritual giants who are aflame with a purpose. . . .

We're a race ready for crusade, for we've recognized that we're a race on this continent that can work out its own salvation. A race must build for nobility of character, for a conquest not on things but on spirit.

We must have a glorified womanhood that can look any man in the face— white, red, yellow, brown, or black and tell of the nobility of character within black womanhood.

Stop making slaves and servants of our women. We've got to stop singing—"Nobody works but father." The Negro mother is doing it all. The women are carrying the burden.

The main reason is that the men lack manhood and energy. They sing too much, "I Can't Give You Anything But Love, Baby." The women can't build homes, rear families off of love alone. The men ought to get down on their knees to Negro women. They've made possible all we have around us— church, home, school, business.

Aspire to be, and all that we are not, God will give us credit for trying.

Source: *Louisiana Weekly*, December 23, 1933. Used with permission.

Joe Louis Wins!

Joe Louis, the son of sharecroppers, became a boxing hero in the Depression decade, winning a number of important bouts and becoming Heavyweight Boxing Cham-

pion of the World in 1937. He was the first African American to hold that title since Jack Johnson in 1907. For many African Americans, Joe Louis's strength and power came to represent their own, and many viewed his victories as theirs. Because a number of his fights put him up against boxers from Germany and Italy just as Nazis and Fascists became increasingly threatening in Europe, Louis also became a symbol of American strength and power. So when Louis defeated Primo Carnera of Italy and Max Baer of Germany in 1935, Americans of all races celebrated.

In 1936 Louis lost against another German, Max Schmeling. But in 1938 the two met again in Yankee Stadium. When Louis, by then Heavyweight Champion of the World, beat Schmeling, Americans once again went wild. He had proven American strength. A black man had triumphed over a German as the Nazis expounded their racist and white supremacist ideology. Just as athlete Jesse Owens demonstrated black ability in front of Hitler in the 1936 Berlin Olympics, Louis moved beyond a racial symbol of pride to become a national symbol as well.

Louis awakened strong emotions in black Americans: race pride, patriotism—and certainly for some, anger at white racism and even perhaps a sense of revenge. Black author Richard Wright, describing the response of Chicago's black community to Louis's victory over Max Baer, emphasized both the joy and the anger African Americans expressed. The Communist Party, whose New Masses newspaper Wright had written the article for, sought to turn black frustration and anger into a revolutionary force to overthrow the system that oppressed them and the entire working class. It is not surprising, then, that Wright highlighted the threat he believed lay beneath that black energy and tied the celebration of Louis's victory to black resentment of white exploitation and discrimination. Other descriptions of Louis's victories usually emphasized the celebration and pride more than the underlying anger. As you read this article, consider not only the description of events, and what it reveals about black community attitudes, but also the way political perspective shapes each writer's analysis of events.

Joe Louis Uncovers Dynamite

"Wun—Tuh—Threee—Fooo—Fiive—Seex—Seven—Eight—Niine-thuun!"

Then:

"JOE LOUIS—THE WINNAH!"

On Chicago's South side five minutes after these words were yelled and Joe Louis' hand was hoisted as victor in his four-round go with Max Baer, Negroes poured out of beer taverns, pool rooms, barber shops, rooming houses, and dingy flats and flooded the streets.

"LOUIS! LOUIS! LOUIS!" they yelled and threw their hats away. They snatched newspapers from the stands of astonished Greeks and tore them up, flinging the bits into the air. They wagged their heads. Lawd, they'd never seen or heard the like of it before. They shook the hands of strangers. They clapped one another on the back. It was like a revival. Really, there was a religious feeling in the air. Well, it wasn't exactly a religious feeling, but it was the *thing*, and you could feel it. It was a feeling of unity, of oneness.

Two hours after the fight the area between South Parkway and Prairie Avenue on 47th Street was jammed with no less than twenty-five thousand Negroes, joy-mad and moving so they didn't know where. Clasping hands they formed long writhing snake-lines and wove in and out of traffic. They seeped out of doorways, oozed from alleys, trickled out of tenements, and flowed down the street, a fluid mass of joy. White storekeepers hastily closed their doors against the tidal wave and stood peeping through plate glass with blanched faces.

Something had happened, all right. And it had happened so confoundingly sudden that the whites in the neighborhood were dumb with fear. They felt—you could see it in their faces—that *something* had ripped loose, exploded. Something which they had long feared and thought was dead. Or if not dead at least so safely buried under the pretense of good-will that they no longer had need to fear it. Where in the world did it come from? And what was worst of all, how far would it go? Say, what's got into these Negroes?

And the whites and the blacks began to *feel* themselves. The blacks began to remember all the little slights and discriminations and insults they had suffered; and their hunger too and their misery. And the whites began to search their souls to see if they had been guilty of something, some time, somewhere, against which this wave of feeling was rising. . . .

Something had popped loose all right. And it had come from deep down. Out of the darkness it had leaped from its coil. And nobody could have said just what it was, and nobody wanted to say. Blacks and whites were afraid. But it was a sweet fear, at least for the blacks. It was a mingling of fear and fulfillment. Something dreaded and yet wanted. . . .

Four centuries of oppression, of frustrated hopes, of black bitterness, felt even in the bones of the bewildered young, were rising to the surface. Yes, unconsciously they had imputed to the brawny image of Joe Louis all the balked dreams of revenge, all the secretly visualized moments of retaliation. AND HE HAD WON! Good Gawd Almighty! Yes, Jesus, it could be done! Didn't Joe do it? You see, Joe was the consciously-felt symbol. He was the concentrated essence of black triumph over white. And it comes so seldom, so seldom. And what could be sweeter than long nourished hate vicariously gratified? From the symbol of Joe's strength they took strength, and in that moment all fear, all obstacles were wiped out, drowned. They stepped out of the mire of hesitation and irresolution and were free! Invincible! A merciless victor over a fallen foe! Yes, they had felt all that—for a moment. . . .

And then the cops came.

Not the carefully picked white cops who were used to batter the skulls of white workers and intellectuals who came to the South Side to march with the black workers to show their solidarity in the struggle against Mussolini's impending invasion of Ethiopia; oh, no, black cops, but trusted black cops and plenty tough. Cops who knew their business, how to handle delicate situations. They piled out of patrols, swinging clubs.

"Git back! Gawddammit, git back!"

But they were very careful, very careful. They didn't hit anybody. They, too, sensed *something*. And they didn't want to trifle with it. And there's no doubt but that they had been instructed not to. Better go easy here. No telling what might happen. They swung clubs, but pushed the crowd back with their hands. . . .

The whites breathed easier. The blood came back to their cheeks.

The Negroes stood on the sidewalks, talking, wondering, looking, breathing hard. They had felt something, and it had been sweet—that feeling. They wanted some more of it, but they were afraid now. The spell was broken.

And about midnight down the street that feeling ebbed, seeping home—flowing back into the beer tavern, the pool room, the café, the barber shop, the dingy flat. Like a sullen river it ran back to its muddy channel, carrying a confused and sentimental memory on its surface, like water-soaked driftwood.

Say, Comrade, here's the wild river that's got to be harnessed and directed. Here's the *something*, that pent-up folk consciousness. Here's a fleeting glimpse of the heart of the Negro, the heart that beats and suffers and hopes—for freedom. Here's that fluid something that's like iron. Here's the real dynamite that Joe Louis uncovered!

Source: Richard Wright, "Joe Louis Uncovers Dynamite," *New Masses*, October 8, 1935. © 1935 Richard Wright, Reprinted by permission of John Hawkins & Associates, Inc.

⁓

The Right to Protest Racial Discrimination

Frustrated by white store owners in black neighborhoods who refused to hire black clerks, and recognizing the political power consumers could wield by boycotting of-

fending stores, black communities around the country launched "Don't Buy Where You Can't Work" campaigns, named after the signs carried by protesters. Store owners, angered at the picket lines these protesters set up outside their stores, convinced local politicians to forbid such demonstrations, claiming they unlawfully interfered with trade. For several years such restrictions stopped the protests and stalled any progress the campaigns had made. But one protest group, the New Negro Alliance, in Washington, D.C., went to court to argue that its pickets were in fact lawful under the 1932 Norris-La Guardia Act (whose provisions were later strengthened by the 1935 National Labor Relations Act). Because the pickets involved an employment issue, Alliance lawyers claimed the protest was protected under the act. In 1938 the Supreme Court agreed with that argument for reasons the justices explain below, and the "Don't Buy" protests resumed. This decision proved a crucial turning point for black activism around the country.

Notice that even the facts were under dispute in this case. Each side presented different claims regarding the Alliance's demands; the justices had to consider whose version of events was closer to the truth, as well as what sorts of employment complaints the law was intended to cover. Note also the arguments and reasoning presented by both the majority of the court and the minority justices who disagreed. Advocates for and opponents of civil rights repeated these positions again and again in the decades that followed.

New Negro Alliance v. Sanitary Grocery Co., 303 U.S. 552 (1938)

NEW NEGRO ALLIANCE et al. v. SANITARY GROCERY CO., Inc.
No. 511.
Argued March 2, 3, 1938.
Decided March 28, 1938.
Mr. Justice ROBERTS delivered the opinion of the Court.

The matter in controversy is whether the case . . . involves or grows out of a labor dispute within the meaning of section 13 of the Norris-La Guardia Act.

The respondent, by bill filed in the District Court of the District of Columbia, sought an injunction restraining the petitioners and their agents from picketing its stores and engaging in other activities injurious to its business. The petitioners answered . . . and an injunction was awarded. The United States Court of Appeals for the District of Columbia affirmed the decree. The importance of the question presented and asserted conflict with the decisions of this and other federal courts moved us to grant certiorari. . . .

The following facts alleged in the bill are admitted: Respondent, a Delaware corporation, operates 255 retail grocery, meat, and vegetable stores, a warehouse and a bakery in the District of Columbia, and employs both white and colored persons. April 3, 1936, it opened a new store at 1936 Eleventh Street N.W., installing personnel having an acquaintance with the trade in the vicinity. Petitioner, the New Negro Alliance, is a corporation composed of colored persons, organized for the mutual improvement of its members and the promotion of civic, educational, benevolent, and charitable enterprises. The individual petitioners are officers of the corporation. The relation of employer and employees does not exist between the respondent and the petitioners or any of them. The petitioners are not engaged in any business competitive with that of the respondent, and the officers, members, or representatives of the Alliance are not engaged in the same business or occupation as the respondent or its employees.

As to other matters of fact, the . . . bill asserts: The petitioners have made arbitrary and summary demands upon the respondent that it engage and employ colored persons in managerial and sales positions in the new store and in various other stores; it is essential to the conduct of the business that respondent employ experienced persons in its stores and compliance with the arbitrary demands of defendants would involve the discharge of white employees and their replacement with colored; it is imperative that respondent be free in the selection and control of persons employed by it without interference by the petitioners or others; petitioners have written respondent letters threatening boycott and ruination of its business and notices that by means of announcements, meetings, and advertising the petitioners will circulate statements that respondent is unfair to colored people and to the colored race and, contrary to fact, that respondent does not employ colored persons; respondent has not acceded to these demands. . . .

The case, then, as it stood for judgment, was this: The petitioners requested the respondent to adopt a policy of employing negro clerks in certain of its stores in the course of personnel changes; the respondent ignored the request and the petitioners caused one person to patrol in front of one of the respondent's stores on one day carrying a placard which said, "Do Your Part! Buy Where You Can Work! No Negroes Employed Here!" and caused or threatened a similar patrol of two other stores of respondent. The information borne by the placard was true. The patrolling did not coerce or intimidate respondent's customers; did not physically obstruct, interfere with, or harass persons desiring to enter the store; the picket acted in an orderly manner, and his conduct did not cause crowds to gather in front of the store. . . .

The Court of Appeals thought that the dispute was not a labor dispute within the Norris-La Guardia Act because it did not involve terms and conditions of employment such as wages, hours, unionization or betterment of working conditions, and that the trial court, therefore, had jurisdiction to issue the injunction. We think the conclusion that the dispute was not a labor dispute within the meaning of the act, because it did not involve terms and conditions of employment in the sense of wages, hours, unionization or betterment of working conditions is erroneous. . . .

The act does not concern itself with the background or the motives of the dispute. The desire for fair and equitable conditions of employment on the part of persons of any race, color, or persuasion, and the removal of discriminations against them by reason of their race or religious beliefs is quite as important to those concerned as fairness and equity in terms and conditions of employment can be to trade or craft unions or any form of labor organization or association. Race discrimination by an employer may reasonably be deemed more unfair and less excusable than discrimination against workers on the ground of union affiliation. There is no justification in the apparent purposes or the express terms of the act for limiting its definition of labor disputes and cases arising therefrom by excluding those which arise with respect to discrimination in terms and conditions of employment based upon differences of race or color. . . .

The legislative history of the act demonstrates that it was the purpose of the Congress further . . . that peaceful and orderly dissemination of information by those defined as persons interested in a labor dispute concerning "terms and conditions of employment" in an industry or a plant or a place of business should be lawful; that, short of fraud, breach of the peace, violence, or conduct otherwise unlawful, those having a direct or indirect interest in such terms and conditions of employment should be at liberty to advertise and disseminate facts and information with respect to terms and conditions of employment, and peacefully to persuade others to concur in their views respecting an employer's practices. The District Court erred in not complying with the provisions of the act.

The decree must be reversed, and the cause remanded to the District Court for further proceedings in conformity with this opinion.

So ordered.

Mr. Justice CARDOZO took no part in the consideration or decision of this case.

Mr. Justice McREYNOLDS (dissenting).

Mr. Justice BUTLER and I cannot accept the view that a "labor dispute" emerges whenever an employer fails to respond to a communication from A, B, and C—irrespective of their race, character, reputation, fitness, previous or present employment—suggesting displeasure because of his choice of employees and their expectation that in the future he will not fail to select men of their complexion.

It seems unbelievable that, in all such circumstances, Congress intended to inhibit courts from extending protection long guaranteed by law and thus, in effect, encourage mobbish interference with the individual's liberty of action. Under the tortured meaning now attributed to the words "labor dispute," no employer—merchant, manufacturer, builder, cobbler, housekeeper or whatnot—who prefers helpers of one color or class can find adequate safeguard against intolerable violations of his freedom if members of some other class, religion, race, or color demand that he give them precedence.

Design thus to promote strife, encourage trespass, and stimulate intimidation, ought not to be admitted where, as here, not plainly avowed. The ultimate result of the view now approved to the very people whom present petitioners claim to represent, it may be, is prefigured by the grievous plight of minorities in lands where the law has become a mere political instrument.

Source: U.S. Supreme Court. *New Negro Alliance v. Sanitary Grocery Co.*, 303 U.S. 552 (1938).

⁓

A 1937 CIO Strike Turns Bloody

While the American Federation of Labor (AFL) did little to aid black workers, and many of its unions excluded them, a small group of industrial unions within the AFL, calling themselves the Committee on Industrial Organization (CIO), began to recruit black members in 1935. The CIO believed that if everyone belonged to the union no one would break a strike, and management would be compelled to negotiate. While some CIO organizers and many of their white union members were racist, their policies did increase the number of black workers willing to join. When the union pursued integration and represented black interests fairly, black workers proved themselves staunch unionists.

One of the most racially progressive groups was the Steel Workers' Organizing Committee (SWOC). It recruited heavily in the Chicago steelyards, and in May 1937, called a strike against the Republic Steel Company for higher wages and union recognition. Most black workers joined their white brothers in each step of the organizing campaign, including the strike. The strike turned bloody, with the company hiring both black and white strike breakers and enlisting police aid in attacking strikers. The worst violence occurred on May 30. That day approximately 5,000 strikers, family members, and union supporters picketed and protested. The police shot into the crowd killing ten men and wounding another nine. Although public opinion placed responsi-

bility on the police and the strike continued for a few more months, in the end workers returned to the plant without a wage increase or union recognition. Most organizing met a similar fate in this decade. Soon after, however, the tide began to turn, and the expansion of unionism benefited millions of black as well as white workers, now committed to interracial labor solidarity.

In this excerpt from their study of Depression-era Chicago, black scholars St. Clair Drake and Horace Cayton describe the events from the perspective of striking black steelworkers.

The Memorial Day Massacre

When the Steel Workers' Organizing Committee (SWOC) called the strike at Republic Steel, more than half of the Negroes in the plant were union members, and these walked out with the white workers. (At the time, about 25,000 men were employed in the plant, of whom 17,000 were white and 8,000 were colored.) Some Negroes did not leave work, however. . . .

A Negro striker reported on his efforts to bring out all of the colored workers:

"We went around and talked to the men that stayed in because it put Negroes in a bad light. Even though many whites stayed in, we colored men felt that those staying in would give Negroes a black eye in the union. You know the first thing white men think is that Negroes will scab and break strikes. We didn't have any success. The men said they needed the money. Most of them were scared of losing their jobs and some are just ignorant."

At one point in the strike, strike-breakers–both white and Negro—were imported by the company. Since most of the colored employees had come out on strike, the union was able to handle the situation in a highly effective manner. One observer told this story:

> The Republic Company had hired a lot of Negroes as strike-breakers, and in order to create racial friction these Negroes had been sent out to break up the picket line—but only when there were all white workers on the picket line. The situation got pretty tense at strike headquarters. There were murmurings of "Niggers are always scabs"; there were little tussles among some of the men.
>
> However, the situation was cleared up in a clever way. All of the Negro strikers stayed near the picket line and waited for a skirmish. When the Negro scabs came out to beat up the pickets, the Negro strikers were let out and gave them such a beating there was never a recurrence of the trouble.

Strike leaders exerted every effort to draw Negroes into full participation at public meetings. . . . An observer described one of these meetings. . . :

> At 2:30, "Spike" Smith, the Negro organizer, announced that a brother from the United Mine Workers of America was there to speak. Another report was

made by . . . a Negro molder. . . . His appearance was greeted with cheers and applause. . . . He owns an automobile which is placed at the disposal of the strikers at all times.

After the speeches, the Negro organizer announced that they had just received a call for a blood transfusion to aid a brother who was in the hospital in a serious condition. (He had been out on the picket line.) He asked for volunteers. At least ten men, two of whom were Negroes, went up . . . without hesitation. . . .

Other methods, too, were used to check racial antagonism. At one meeting, Spike addressed a mixed audience, and denounced "the ignorant Negro who held a gun on the workers," citing this as "an old company technique to incite racial prejudice." He cried out, "A scab is a scab, black or white, and should be scorned by all union members, black and white!" He insisted that today "workers refuse to bite at the racial bait-line." Whistles and cheers followed his speech.

A special effort was made to involve Negro women in strike activities. . . .

The climax of the Republic strike came with the "Memorial Day Massacre." . . . [One] Negro striker . . . gave a dramatic account of the police attack:

On that Sunday we marched out of the plant with signs. Lots of us were singing songs and laughing. I was in the front line. All of a sudden the cops started shooting. When they started, I ran to my extreme right, then west, then I made an "L" turn to the south. All the time, bullets were going right past my face.

When I looked up I saw a guy right on top of the plant training his gun on us. I couldn't tell whether it was a machine gun, 'cause I was anxious to get out of the line of fire. I could see the police in my path, the way I was running, so I turned around toward Sam's Place. I ran to a car and started to duck in it. A bullet whizzed by. . . Boy, I shake now when I think that if I hadn't ducked I'd have been shot in the head. . . .

The CIO regards the men who died that day as martyrs to the union cause. Among the ten men killed was one Negro. After being shot, he was beaten by the police and taken to jail. Later his wife had him removed to a private hospital, where he died. She seemed bewildered by this outburst of violence resulting in her husband's death. This is how she talked about it:

He was told to go to the meeting that Sunday. He was on the front line and was one of the first to get hurt. I have his clothes here. You can see where he was shot in the back. His hat is bloody. He sure was beat terrible. His life was really lost for the CIO, whether he understood it or not. I do hope his loss will help others who live. . . .

I guess a union's all right, but when people have to lose their life it ain't so good. 'Course, in war, men lose their lives for freedom, but this is a little different. The union caused me to lose a very good husband. . . .

Those Negro members who continued to support the union after the "Memorial Day Massacre" felt that the CIO was fair to them as Negroes, and that the strike was justified.

Source: Excerpt from "Democracy and Economic Necessity: Black Workers and the New Unions," in *Black Metropolis: a Study of Negro Life in a Northern City*, copyright 1945 by St. Clair Drake and Horace R. Cayton and renewed, 1973, by St. Clair Drake and Susan Woodson, reprinted by permission of Houghton Mifflin Harcourt Publishing Company.

⌢

To End Employment Discrimination

When World War II began, the U.S. was not yet a combatant. Still, President Roosevelt indirectly declared war on the Axis powers by proclaiming that America was the "arsenal of democracy." The resulting expansion of military expansion revived the U.S. economy and ended the Depression. It did not end for African Americans, however, who continued to suffer from racism and discrimination. They were once again "last hired." Black leaders, determined to increase employment opportunities for black workers, met in 1941 at Harlem's Hotel Theresa. They agreed to demand that the government enforce equal access to employment and integrate the Armed Forces. Labor leader A. Philip Randolph threatened to bring thousands of black protesters to Washington, D.C., in a "March on Washington" if the president did not yield to these demands.

As Roosevelt struggled to generate support for the war effort, he concluded that any public protest would undercut his assertions that the nation was united against Fascism. Roosevelt sent his wife, Eleanor, and Mayor Fiorello La Guardia of New York, both strong advocates of black civil rights, to try to persuade Randolph to call off the march. When they failed, the president issued Executive Order 8802 in June 1941. The order met some, but not all, of the group's demands. It prohibited discrimination by any employer receiving a government contract, but the mechanisms for enforcement were weak. Nor did Roosevelt integrate the Armed Forces. In response Randolph called off the march, but urged African Americans to continue their struggle until the full agenda of the March on Washington was fulfilled. Roosevelt's executive order prohibited discrimination in any industry receiving government defense contracts and established the Committee on Fair Employment Practice to monitor compliance. In a 1942 article, Randolph explains the ongoing mission of the March on Washington Movement to extend the antidiscriminatory measures of the executive order and expand integration into all areas of public and civic life. Notice that Randolph called for an all-black movement—not because he opposed interracial cooperation, but to highlight black power and black unity.

Executive Order 8802
Reaffirming Policy of Full Participation in the Defense Program by All Persons, Regardless of Race, Creed, Color, or National Origin, and Directing Certain Action in Furtherance of Said Policy

WHEREAS it is the policy of the United States to encourage full participation in the national defense program by all citizens of the United States, regardless of race, creed, color, or national origin, in the firm belief that the democratic way of life within the Nation can be defended successfully only with the help and support of all groups within its borders; and

WHEREAS there is evidence that available and needed workers have been barred from employment in industries engaged in defense production solely because of considerations of race, creed, color, or national origin, to the detriment of workers' morale and of national unity:

NOW, THEREFORE, by virtue of the authority vested in me by the Constitution and the statutes, and as a prerequisite to the successful conduct of our national defense production effort, I do hereby reaffirm the policy of the United States that there shall be no discrimination in the employment of workers in defense industries or government because of race, creed, color, or national origin, and I do hereby declare that it is the duty of employers and of labor organizations, in furtherance of said policy and of this order, to provide for the full and equitable participation of all workers in defense industries, without discrimination because of race, creed, color, or national origin;

And it is hereby ordered as follows:

1. All departments and agencies of the Government of the United States concerned with vocational and training programs for defense production shall take special measures appropriate to assure that such programs are administered without discrimination because of race, creed, color, or national origin;
2. All contracting agencies of the Government of the United States shall include in all defense contracts hereafter negotiated by them a provi-

sion obligating the contractor not to discriminate against any worker because of race, creed, color, or national origin;

3. There is established in the Office of Production Management a Committee on Fair Employment Practice, which shall consist of a chairman and four other members to be appointed by the President. . . . The Committee shall receive and investigate complaints of discrimination in violation of the provisions of this order and shall take appropriate steps to redress grievances which it finds to be valid. The Committee shall also recommend to the several departments and agencies of the Government of the United States and to the President all measures which may be deemed by it necessary or proper to effectuate the provisions of this order.

Franklin D. Roosevelt
The White House,
June 25, 1941.

The March on Washington Movement: "Why Should We March?"

Though I have found no Negroes who want to see the United Nations lose this war, I have found many who, before the war ends, want to see the stuffing knocked out of white supremacy and of empire over subject peoples. American Negroes, involved as we are in the general issues of the conflict, are confronted not with a choice but with the challenge both to win democracy for ourselves at home and to help win the war for democracy the world over. . . .

For if the war for democracy is not won abroad, the fight for democracy cannot be won at home. If this war cannot be won for the white peoples, it will not be won for the darker races.

Conversely, if freedom and equality are not vouchsafed for the peoples of color, the war for democracy will not be won. Unless this double-barreled thesis is accepted and applied, the darker races will never wholeheartedly fight for the victory of the United Nations. That is why those familiar with the thinking of the American Negro have sensed his lack of enthusiasm. . . .

That is why questions are being raised by Negroes in church, labor union and fraternal society; in poolroom, barbershop, schoolroom, hospital, hairdressing parlor; on college campus, railroad, and bus. One can hear such questions asked as these: What have Negroes to fight for? What's the difference between Hitler and that "cracker" Talmadge of Georgia? Why has a man got to be Jim Crowed to die for democracy? If you haven't got democracy yourself, how can you carry it to somebody else?

What are the reasons for this state of mind? The answer is: discrimination, segregation, Jim Crow. . . . Vested political interests in race prejudice are so deeply entrenched that to them winning the war against Hitler is secondary to preventing Negroes from winning democracy for themselves. . . . While labor, business, and farm are subjected to ceilings and floors and not allowed to carry on as usual, these interests trade in the dangerous business of race hate as usual.

When the defense program began and billions of the taxpayers' money were appropriated for guns, ships, tanks, and bombs, Negroes presented themselves for work only to be given the cold shoulder. North as well as South, and despite their qualifications, Negroes were denied skilled employment. Not until their wrath and indignation took the form of a proposed protest march on Washington, scheduled for July 1, 1941, did things begin to move in the form of defense jobs for Negroes. The march was postponed by the timely issuance . . . of the famous Executive Order No. 8802 by President Roosevelt. But this order and the President's Committee on Fair Employment Practice, established thereunder, have as yet only scratched the surface by way of eliminating discriminations on account of race or color in war industry. Both management and labor unions in too many places and in too many ways are still drawing the color line.

It is to meet this situation squarely with direct action that the March on Washington Movement launched its present program of protest mass meetings. Twenty thousand were in attendance at Madison Square Garden, June 16; sixteen thousand in the Coliseum in Chicago, June 26; nine thousand in the City Auditorium of St. Louis, August 14. Meetings of such magnitude were unprecedented among Negroes. The vast throngs were drawn from all walks and levels of Negro life—businessmen, teachers, laundry workers, Pullman porters, waiters, and red caps; preachers, crapshooters, and social workers; jitterbugs and Ph.D.'s. They came and sat in silence, thinking, applauding only when they considered the truth was told, when they felt strongly that something was going to be done about it.

The March on Washington Movement is essentially a movement of the people. It is all Negro and pro-Negro, but not for that reason anti-white or anti-Semitic, or anti-Catholic, or anti-foreign, or anti-labor. Its major weapon is the non-violent demonstration of Negro mass power. Negro leadership has united back of its drive for jobs and justice. "Whether Negroes should march on Washington, and if so, when?" will be the focus of a forthcoming national conference. For the plan of a protest march has not been abandoned. Its purpose would be to demonstrate that American Negroes are in deadly earnest, and all out for their full rights. No power on earth can cause them today to abandon their fight to wipe out every vestige of second class citizenship and the dual standards that plague them.

A community is democratic only when the humblest and weakest person can enjoy the highest civil, economic, and social rights that the biggest and most powerful possess. To trample on these rights of both Negroes and poor whites is such a commonplace in the South that it takes readily to anti-social, anti-labor, anti-Semitic and anti-Catholic propaganda. . . . Oppression of the Negroes in the United States, like suppression of the Jews in Germany, may open the way for a fascist dictatorship.

By fighting for their rights now, American Negroes are helping to make America a moral and spiritual arsenal of democracy. Their fight against the poll tax, against lynch law, segregation and Jim Crow, their fight for economic, political and social equality, thus becomes part of the global war for freedom.

Program of the March on Washington Movement
1. We demand, in the interest of national unity, the abrogation of every law which makes a distinction in treatment between citizens based on religion, creed, color, or national origin. This means an end to Jim Crow in education, in housing, in transportation and in every other social, economic, and political privilege; and especially, we demand, in the capital of the nation, an end to all segregation in public places and in public institutions.
2. We demand legislation to enforce the Fifth and Fourteenth Amendments guaranteeing that no person shall be deprived of life, liberty or property without due process of law, so that the full weight of the national government may be used for the protection of life and thereby may end the disgrace of lynching.
3. We demand the enforcement of the Fourteenth and Fifteenth Amendments and the enactment of the Pepper Poll Tax bill so that all barriers in the exercise of suffrage are eliminated.
4. We demand the abolition of segregation and discrimination in the army, navy, marine corps, air corps, and all other branches of national defense.
5. We demand an end to discrimination in jobs and job training. Further, we demand that the F.E.P.C. be made a permanent administrative agency of the U.S. Government and that it be given power to enforce its decisions based on its findings.
6. We demand that federal funds be withheld from any agency which practices discrimination in the use of such funds.

7. We demand colored and minority group representation on all administrative agencies so that these groups may have recognition of their democratic right to participate in formulating policies.

8. We demand representation for the colored and minority racial groups on all missions, political and technical, which will be sent to the peace conference so that the interests of all people everywhere may be fully recognized and justly provided for in the post-war settlement.

Source: A. Philip Randolph, "Why Should We March?" *Survey Graphic* 31, no. 11 (November 1942): 488–89.

~

Bibliography

For ease of use, this bibliography has been divided into thematic sections, each with a brief description and an alphabetical list of books. In each case, the books selected are well regarded and current. Nevertheless, there are dozens of other worthy books that could be added; students should consider this bibliography a launching pad rather than a complete list of sources.

Some of the most important sources of information about African Americans during the Great Depression come from the period itself. These fall into three types: oral histories and memoirs of those active at the time; reports by government bodies; and results of contemporary scholarly research. Several of each type are offered here. In many cases their topics overlap with the categories below. They are collected here, however, to highlight their importance as sources that come directly from the time period under study.

Important oral histories and memoirs include Elizabeth Davey and Rodney Clark, *Remember My Sacrifice: The Autobiography of Clinton Clark, Tenant Farm Organizer and Early Civil Rights Activist* (2007); Federal Writers' Project, *These Are Our Lives: As Told by the People and Written by Members of the Federal Writers' Project of the Works Progress Administration in North Carolina, Tennessee and Georgia* (1939); Constance Baker Motley, *Equal Justice Under Law: An Autobiography* (1998); Nell Painter, *The Narrative of Hosea Hudson: His Life as a Negro Communist in the South* (1979); Theodore Rosengarten, *All God's Dangers: the Life of Nate Shaw* (1974); Walter White, *A Rising Wind* (1945); Roy Wilkins, *Standing Fast: The Autobiography of Roy Wilkins* (1994); and Richard Wright, *Black Boy: A Record of Childhood and Youth* (1945; 2007).

Research done by scholars during the Depression on race or African American experience include Horace Mann Bond, *The Education of the Negro in the American*

Social Order (1934); St. Clair Drake and Horace Cayton, *Black Metropolis: A Study of Negro Life in a Northern City* (1945, 1993); Claude McKay, *Harlem: Negro Metropolis* (1940); Gunnar Myrdal, *An American Dilemma: The Negro Problem and Modern Democracy* (1944, 1996); Roi Ottley, *New World A-Coming: Inside Black America* (1943); Arnold Rose, *The Negro in America: The Condensed Version of Gunnar Myrdal's An American Dilemma* (1948); Sterling Spero and Abram Harris, *The Black Worker* (1931); Richard Sterner, *The Negro's Share: A Study of Income, Consumption, Housing and Public Assistance* (1943); Thomas Woofter Jr., *Negro Problems in Cities: A Study* (1928, 1969); and Richard Wright, *Twelve Million Black Voices* (1941, 2002).

Finally, some primary sources come in the form of organizational reports, such as David Carlton and Peter Coclanis, eds., *Confronting Southern Poverty in the Great Depression: The Report on Economic Conditions of the South with Related Documents* (1996); Children's Bureau, *White House Conference on Children in a Democracy, Final Report, 1940* (1940), and *Report of the National Conference on the Problems of the Negro and Negro Youth* (1937); and Doxey Wilkerson, *Special Problems in Negro Education* (1939).

The experiences of African Americans in the Depression and New Deal have remained a fascination for historians. A number of excellent overviews were written some time ago but they remain important to any study of the period. Some of the best are Melvin Dubofsky, ed., *Women and Minorities during the Great Depression and the New Deal* (1990); John Kirby, *Black Americans in the Roosevelt Era: Liberalism and Race* (1980); Harvard Sitkoff, *A New Deal for Blacks: The Emergence of Civil Rights as a National Issue: The Depression Decade* (1978); Bernard Sternsher, ed., *The Negro in Depression and War: Prelude to Revolution, 1930–1945* (1969); and Raymond Wolters, *Negroes and the Great Depression: The Problem of Economic Recovery* (1974).

Several works focus on the South during the Depression. See Anthony Badger, *New Deal/New South: An Anthony J. Badger Reader* (2007); Roger Biles, *The South and the New Deal* (1994); David Brown and Clive Webb, *Race in the American South: From Slavery to Civil Rights* (2007); Jack T. Kirby, *Rural Worlds Lost: The American South 1920–1960* (1986); and Douglas Smith, *The New Deal in the Urban South* (1988).

The Great Depression was, in the end, economic, and a number of scholarly books have examined economic and labor issues from the perspective of race. Inextricable from these discussions, of course, is trade union organizing, which found new possibilities and new energy in this period. Among the dozens of excellent books on these subjects include Eric Arnesen, *The Black Worker: Race, Labor, and Civil Rights Since Emancipation* (2007), and *Brotherhoods of Color: Black Railroad Workers and the Struggle for Equality* (2002); Beth T. Bates, *Pullman Porters and the Rise of Protest Politics in Black America 1925–1945* (2000); Donald Grubbs, *Cry from the Cotton: The Southern Tenant Farmers' Union and the New Deal* (1999); Rick Halpern, *Down on the Killing Floor: Black and White Workers in Chicago's Packinghouses 1904–54* (1997); Darlene Clark Hine, *Black Women in White: Racial Conflict and Cooperation in the Nursing Profession 1890–1950* (1989); Michael Honey, *Southern Labor and Black Civil Rights: Or-*

ganizing Memphis Workers (1993); Roger Horowitz, *Negro and White, Unite and Fight! A Social History of Industrial Unionism in Meatpacking 1930–90* (1997); Robert Korstad, *Civil Rights Unionism: Tobacco Workers and the Struggle for Democracy in the Mid-Twentieth Century* (2003); David Lewis-Colman, *Race against Liberalism: Black Workers and the UAW in Detroit* (2008); Bruce Nelson, *Divided We Stand: American Workers and the Struggle for Black Equality* (2001); Henry Louis Taylor Jr. and Walter Hill, eds., *Historical Roots of the Urban Crisis: African Americans in the Industrial City 1900–1950* (2000); and Robert Weems Jr., *Black Business in the Black Metropolis: The Chicago Metropolitan Assurance Company 1924–1985* (1996).

Beyond labor organizing, the era is particularly notable for the tremendous engagement by African Americans in political action on the federal, state, and local levels. Individual political leaders and political organizations concerned with race actively pursued racial justice within the framework of the New Deal. Others pursued more radical political changes. In addition to electoral politics, many reformers and radicals also took to the streets in more direct action.

Works that consider race and politics include Michael Brown, *Race, Money and the American Welfare State* (1999); Jane Daily, Glenda Gilmore, and Bryant Simon, eds, *Jumpin' Jim Crow: Southern Politics from Civil War to Civil Rights* (2000); John Egerton, *Speak Now against the Day: The Generation Before the Civil Rights Movement* (1994); Adam Fairclough, *Better Day Coming: Blacks and Equality, 1890–2000* (2001), and *Race and Democracy: The Civil Rights Struggle in Louisiana, 1915–1972* (2008); Kevin Gaines, *Uplifting the Race: Black Leadership, Politics and Culture in the Twentieth Century* (1996); Doug McAdam, *Political Process and the Development of Black Insurgency 1930–1970* (1982); Mary Poole, *The Segregated Origins of Social Security: African Americans and the Welfare State* (2006); Patricia Sullivan, *Days of Hope: Race and Democracy in the New Deal Era* (1996); and Nancy Weiss, *Farewell to the Party of Lincoln: Black Politics in the Age of FDR* (1983). Nancy Grant, *TVA and Black Americans: Planning for the Status Quo* (1990), examines a specific New Deal program and its impact on the black community in the region.

Others focus on specific organizations or individuals. Those looking at liberal groups or leaders include Hayward Farrar, *The Baltimore Afro-American: 1892–1950* (1998); Joyce Hanson, *Mary McLeod Bethune and Black Women's Political Action* (2003); Jonathan Holloway, *Confronting the Veil: Abram Harris, Jr., E. Franklin Frazier, and Ralph Bunche 1919–1941* (2001); Nina Mjagkij, *Light in the Darkness: African Americans and the YMCA 1852–1946* (1994); Dennis Nordin, *The New Deal's Black Congressman: a Life of Arthur Wergs Mitchell* (1997); Linda Reed, *Simple Democracy and Common Sense: The Southern Conference Movement 1938–1963* (1991); and Toure Reed, *Not Alms but Opportunity: The Urban League and the Politics of Racial Uplift 1910–1950* (2008).

A number of books examine radicals, radicalism, and the left, such as Jervis Anderson, *Bayard Rustin: Troubles I've Seen* (1996); Glenda Gilmore, *Defying Dixie: The Radical Roots of Civil Rights 1919–1950* (2008); Gerald Horne, *Black Liberation/Red Scare: Ben Davis and Communist Party* (1993); Robin D. G. Kelley, *Hammer and Hoe: Alabama*

Communists during the Great Depression (1990); William Maxwell, *New Negro, Old Left* (1999); Bill Mullen, *Popular Fronts: Chicago and African-American Cultural Politics 1935–46* (1999); Mark Naison, *Communists in Harlem During the Great Depression* (1983); and Mark Solomon, *The Cry Was Unity: Communists and African Americans 1917–1936* (1998). Often considered radical was black nationalism, explored in William Van Deburg, *Modern Black Nationalism: from Marcus Garvey to Louis Farrakhan* (1997).

Legal protests have received a great deal of attention. See Kevin Janken, *White: The Biography of Walter White, Mr. NAACP* (2003); Richard Kluger, *Simple Justice: The History of "Brown v. Board of Education" and Black America's Struggle for Equality* (1976); Genna Rae McNeil, *Groundwork: Charles Hamilton Houston and the Struggle for Civil Rights* (1983); Mark Tushnet, *Making Civil Rights Law: Thurgood Marshall and the Supreme Court 1935–1961* (1994), and *The NAACP's Legal Strategy against Segregated Educated Education 1925–1950* (1987); and Juan Williams, *Thurgood Marshall: American Revolutionary* (1998).

While national overviews are always useful, different cities and communities experienced the hardship of the Depression, the day-to-day workings of the New Deal, and the impact of political organizing in distinct ways. Community studies can provide more in-depth analysis of the period through their narrower geographic focus. These studies of communities range across the country, rural and urban, large and small: Charles Banner-Haley, *To Do Good and to Do Well: Middle Class Blacks and the Depression, Philadelphia, 1929–1941* (1993); Elizabeth R. Bethel, *Promiseland: A Century of Life in a Negro Community* (1981); Albert Broussard, *Black San Francisco: The Struggle for Racial Equality in the West 1900–1954* (1993); Dominic Capeci, *Race Relations in Wartime Detroit: The Sojourner Truth Housing Controversy of 1942* (1984); Charles Coulter, *Taking Up the Black Man's Burden: Kansas City's African American Communities 1865–1939* (2006); Karen Ferguson, *Black Politics in New Deal Atlanta* (2001); Douglas Flamming, *Bound for Freedom: Black Los Angeles in Jim Crow America* (2005); Cheryl Greenberg, *"Or Does It Explode?" Black Harlem in the Great Depression* (1990); Randal Jelks, *African Americans in the Furniture City: The Struggle for Civil Rights in Grand Rapids* (2006); Jennifer Lemak, *Southern Life, Northern City: The History of Albany's Rapp Road Community* (2008); Earl Lewis, *In Their Own Interests: Race, Class and Power in Twentieth Century Norfolk, Virginia* (1991); Shirley Moore, *To Place Our Deeds: The African American Community in Richmond, California 1910–1963* (2000); H. Viscount Nelson, *Black Leadership's Response to the Great Depression in Philadelphia* (2006); Richard Pierce, *Polite Protest: The Political Economy of Race in Indianapolis, 1920–1970* (2005); Quintard Taylor, *The Forging of a Black Community: Seattle's Central District from 1870 Through the Civil Rights Era* (1994); Richard Thomas, *Life for Us Is What We Make It: Building Black Community in Detroit 1915–1945* (1992); Joe Trotter Jr., *Black Milwaukee: The Making of an Industrial Proletariat 1915–1945* (2007), and his edited volume, *The Great Migration in Historical Perspective: New Dimensions of Race, Class, and Gender* (1991); and Victoria Wolcott, *Remaking Respectability: African American Women in Interwar Detroit* (2001).

Hundreds of books offer biographical overviews of specific artists and writers. Here instead are listed works focusing more broadly on African Americans in the arts and the impact of black culture on American art: Romare Bearden and Harry Henderson, *A History of African-American Artists: From 1792 to the Present* (1992); Donald Bogle, *Toms, Coons, Mulattoes, Mammies & Bucks: An Interpretive History of Blacks in American Films* (2001); Lisa Collins and Lisa Messinger, *African-American Artists 1929–1945: Prints, Drawings, and Paintings in the Metropolitan Museum of Art* (2003); Scott DeVeaux, *BeBop: A Social and Musical History* (1997); Manthia Diawara, ed., *Black American Cinema* (1993); Melvin Patrick Ely, *The Adventures of Amos 'N' Andy: A Social History of an American Phenomenon* (1991); Rena Fraden, *Blueprints for a Black Federal Theatre* (1994); Glenda Gill, *White Grease Paint on Black Performers: A Study of the Federal Theatre 1935–1939* (1988); Ed Guerrero, *Framing Blackness: The African American Image in Film* (1993); Michael Harris, *Colored Pictures: Race and Visual Representation* (2006); Robin D. G. Kelley, *Race Rebels: Culture, Politics and the Black Working Class* (1994); Susan Manning, *Modern Dance Negro Dance: Race in Motion* (2004); Stacy Morgan, *Rethinking Social Realism: African American Art and Literature 1930–1953* (2004); Nicholas Natanson, *The Black Image in the New Deal: The Politics of FSA Photography* (1992); Jesse Rhines, *Black Film/White Money* (1996); Cedrick Robinson, *Forgeries of Memory and Meaning: Blacks and the Regimes of Race in American Theater and Film before World War II* (2007); and James Smethurst, *The New Red Negro: The Literary Left and African American Poetry 1930–1946* (1999).

Examinations of foreign policy and the black community remind us that racial issues are global. See, for example, Joseph Harris, *African American Reactions to War in Ethiopia 1936–1941* (1994); James Meriwether, *Proudly We Can Be Africans: Black Americans and Africa 1935–1961* (2001); Brenda Gayle Plummer, *Rising Wind: Black Americans and U.S. Foreign Affairs 1935–1960* (1996); William Scott, *The Sons of Sheba's Race: African Americans and the Italo-Ethiopian War 1935–1941* (1993); and Penny Von Eschen, *Race Against Empire: Black Americans and Anticolonialism 1937–1957* (1997).

Among the thousands of books on other topics in Depression-era African American history are several worth noting here, ranging from sports to religion, prison to lynching, social policy to suburbanization, teaching to medicine. Religion is explored in Wallace Best, *Passionately Human, No Less Divine: Religion and Culture in Black Chicago 1915–1952* (2007); Claude Clegg III, *An Original Man: The Life and Times of Elijah Muhammad* (1997); Jill Watts, *God, Harlem, USA: The Father Divine Story* (1992); and Robert Weisbrot, *Father Divine and the Struggle for Racial Equality* (1983). Several works consider science, medicine, psychology, and race including James Jones, *Bad Blood: The Tuskegee Syphilis Experiment* (1981); Spencie Love, *One Blood: The Death and Resurrection of Charles R. Drew* (1996); and Daryl Scott, *Contempt and Pity: Social Policy and the Image of the Damaged Black Psyche 1880–1996* (1997). Race and justice are explored in James McGovern, *Anatomy of a Lynching: The Killing of Claude Neal* (1982) and David Oshinsky, *Worse than Slavery: Parchman Farm and the*

Ordeal of Jim Crow Justice (1997). Richard Bak examines race through sports with *Joe Louis: The Great Black Hope* (1998). Adam Fairclough looks at race and education in *A Class of Their Own: Black Teachers in the Segregated South* (2007). Finally, Andrew Weise examines the intersections of race and residence in *Places of Their Own: African American Suburbanization in the Twentieth Century* (2005).

Index

~

About the Author

Cheryl Greenberg is the Paul E. Raether Distinguished Professor of History at Trinity College in Hartford, CT. She has published several books: *Troubling the Waters: Black-Jewish Relations in the American Century* (2006); *Black Harlem in the Great Depression* (1991), and *"Or Does It Explode?"*; Editor, *A Circle of Trust: Remembering SNCC* (1998).